TWIN TRANSFORMATION

TWIN TRANSFORMATION

A Gripping Tale of How
AI and Sustainability Converge,
and the Race to Get It Right

Michael Wade

Konstantinos Trantopoulos

To Heidi... My favorite distraction and greatest inspiration.

Michael Wade

To my family - immediate, extended, chosen.

Konstantinos Trantopoulos

Contents

PREFACE	10
CAST OF CHARACTERS	5
PROLOGUE	13
ACT 1: ARRIVAL AND RESISTANCE	**17**
CHAPTER 1: A COMPANY AT A CROSSROADS	19
CHAPTER 2: A BOARD MANDATE FOR A TWIN TRANSFORMATION	23
CHAPTER 3: NEW HIRES	29
CHAPTER 4: A FRAGMENTED LANDSCAPE	39
CHAPTER 5: RESISTANCE FROM WITHIN	43
Transformation Takeaways: Memo to Leadership	48
ACT 2: EARLY CHALLENGES	**53**
CHAPTER 6: BUILDING AN AI SUSTAINABILITY FOUNDATION	55
CHAPTER 7: THE BOARDROOM BATTLE	61
CHAPTER 8: THE AI-POWERED PILOT BEGINS	67
CHAPTER 9: THE PILOT'S GROWING PAINS	73
CHAPTER 10: A BREAKTHROUGH IN THE MARKET	79
CHAPTER 11: CUSTOMER RESISTANCE	93
CHAPTER 12: THE BOARD'S ULTIMATUM	101
Transformation Takeaways: Memo to Leadership	106
ACT 3: TURNING THE TIDE	**109**
CHAPTER 13: THE PUSH FOR QUICK WINS	111
CHAPTER 14: THE PUBLIC RELATIONS SETBACK	115
CHAPTER 15: CRISIS OF CONFIDENCE	121
CHAPTER 16: WINNING THE WORKFORCE	125
CHAPTER 17: THE POWER STRUGGLE	133
CHAPTER 18: THE RECKONING	137
CHAPTER 19: BREAKING THE AI BARRIER	141
CHAPTER 20: LEADERSHIP SHAKE-UP	147
Transformation Takeaways: Memo To Leadership	151
ACT 4: VICTORY AND THE ROAD AHEAD	**155**
CHAPTER 21: THE TRANSFORMATION OF THERMADYNAMICS	157

CHAPTER 22: AI AND THE CIRCULAR ECONOMY	163
CHAPTER 23: CUSTOMER BEHAVIOR	169
CHAPTER 24: SCALING FOR THE FUTURE	175
CHAPTER 25: A MARKET RESURGENCE	183
CHAPTER 26: THE FUTURE IS HERE	189
Transformation Takeaways: Memo To Leadership	195
EPILOGUE: THE MERCURY PRIZE	199
ABOUT THE AUTHORS	207

Preface

Why a Business Novel?

When we set out to write *Twin Transformation*, we were driven by a simple conviction: most business books fail to capture the human drama at the heart of real organizational change. In their quest to be rigorous, factual, and serious, many end up feeling distant, dry, and detached from the lived experiences of those who drive and endure transformation. We chose to write this book as a business novel because we wanted to reflect the messiness and richness of real-world change.

In practice, facts are rarely clear-cut. Motivations are often mixed, and resistance doesn't always follow a rational script. The fictional format gave us the freedom to portray this reality, rather than the sanitized, linear versions you find in case studies or white papers. Transformation is not just about spreadsheets, profit margins, and quarterly results. It is a deeply human story, woven from ambition, innovation, fear, resistance, hope, and the relentless pursuit of a better future.

As scholars, educators, and practitioners, we have spent years immersed in the worlds of strategy, technology, and organizational change. We have seen firsthand that numbers and frameworks, while important, can only go so far in explaining why transformations succeed or fail. What truly drives change, or stalls it, is often found in the tensions, conversations, and decisions made by people under pressure.

By choosing the business novel as our format, we aimed to bring these dynamics to life. Our hope is that this story not only informs but resonates, challenges, and inspires. We want readers to see themselves in the characters, reflect on their own experiences, and engage with ideas in a way that feels both grounded and energizing. After all, the future of business is not just something to analyze; it is something we all have to live, lead, and shape.

All characters and situations in this book are fictional. However, they are inspired by the real people, challenges, and transformations we have encountered through our teaching, consulting, and research.

AI and Sustainability: A Twin Transformation

At the core of this book are the twin forces of artificial intelligence and sustainability. Our motivation began with a question we couldn't shake: How can artificial intelligence reshape sustainability, not as a compliance headache, but as a competitive advantage? We saw companies like ThermaDynamics everywhere - corporate giants facing disruption from nimble startups, regulatory pressures for greener operations, and a market demanding smarter, more intelligent solutions.

Too often, sustainability is seen as an obligation, a box to check to satisfy regulators and investors. But what if it could be something more? What if AI could turn sustainability from a burden into a driver of efficiency, cost savings, and new business opportunities?

That's the vision we explore in this book. AI and sustainability aren't just parallel trends; they are two forces that, when combined, can unlock unprecedented value. AI's ability to optimize processes, predict inefficiencies, and automate decision-making has the potential to transform sustainability from a cost center into a business accelerator. Whether it's reducing waste, optimizing energy use, creating more resilient supply chains, or designing intelligent, low-carbon products, AI can do more than just help companies meet ESG targets. It can make them more profitable, resilient, and innovative in the process. And through that, it can contribute to a better planet, one where economic growth and sustainability are not at odds but mutually reinforcing forces that drive long-term prosperity.

Through the journey of ThermaDynamics, we show how these forces collide, clash, and ultimately converge into a new model of industry leadership. But we also illuminate the human side of transformation, like the resistance from those who fear losing control, the breakthroughs that come from unexpected collaborations, and the courage it takes to bet on a vision when the odds seem stacked against you.

This business novel is our tribute to the power of storytelling in business. We've written numerous articles and books filled with data and frameworks, but stories have a unique ability to connect, persuade, and inspire. By crafting the tale of Elena Navarro, Vikram Mehta, Thomas Greaves, and their colleagues at ThermaDynamics, we aim to create a narrative that mirrors the real-world struggles and triumphs of today's leaders.

Finally, we wrote *Twin Transformation* for you, the reader, the thinker, the dreamer who believes that business can be a force for good in the world. Our hope is that this story not only entertains you but provokes reflection and equips you with fresh perspectives on leading change in an era defined by complexity and uncertainty. Whether you're strategizing in a boardroom, innovating in a startup garage, or exploring ideas in a classroom, we invite you to step into the world of ThermaDynamics, wrestle with its challenges, reflect on its lessons, and imagine what's possible in your own journey of transformation.

Acknowledgments

This book would not have been possible without the inspiration and insights from the many business leaders, researchers, and entrepreneurs who are actively shaping the intersection of artificial intelligence and sustainability. We are deeply grateful to the professionals who generously shared their experiences, the colleagues who challenged our thinking, and the countless innovators who continue to push boundaries in their own organizations.

We are especially thankful to Julia Binder, Knut Haanaes and Amit Joshi, whose deep expertise in sustainability and AI enriched and sharpened many of the ideas explored in this book. Their perspectives helped anchor our narrative in the realities of today's sustainability and AI challenges and opportunities.

Our sincere thanks also go to Esteban Mezzano, whose careful reading and insightful comments greatly influenced the final manuscript. Many of his thoughtful suggestions have found their way into these pages.

We are indebted to Heidi Bjerkan, whose legendary attention to detail elevated the clarity and precision of the text. Her editorial support has been second to none.

A special thank you goes to Tima Jadaan, who skillfully guided this project from its earliest outlines through the complex process of publication. Her steady hand, sound judgment, and unwavering commitment were invaluable throughout.

Finally, to our families and friends, thank you for your patience, encouragement, and enduring belief in this project. Writing a book is never a solo journey, and we are profoundly grateful to have had your support every step of the way.

With gratitude,
Michael Wade & Konstantinos Trantopoulos

June 2025

Cast of Characters

Elena Navarro

Elena Navarro brings environmental expertise and a pragmatic business sense to her role as Chief Sustainability Officer at ThermaDynamics. The forty-nine-year-old was educated at the Universidad Autónoma de Madrid and the London School of Economics, but it was her decade at the Global Sustainability Initiative, an NGO, that truly defined her approach to environmental change.

At GSI, Navarro evolved from idealist to sophisticated negotiator, working from Brazilian rainforests to Southeast Asian industrial zones. She built her reputation creating practical sustainability frameworks that corporations could implement while maintaining environmental integrity.

Navarro carries herself with confidence and is gifted at explaining complex concepts through real-world examples. Her only personal adornment is a silver tree pendant – a gift from an indigenous Brazilian community. Despite her NGO background, she speaks business language fluently, framing sustainability in terms of risk, opportunity, and ROI.

Her greatest strength is finding balance between idealism and pragmatism, seeing innovation opportunities where others see conflicts between environmental protection and business growth.

The move to ThermaDynamics marks her first corporate role.

Vikram Mehta

At thirty-eight, Vikram Mehta joins ThermaDynamics as Chief AI Officer with impressive Silicon Valley credentials and a drive for meaningful technological impact. Born in Bangalore and educated at IIT and Stanford, his journey took him from coding in his parents' garage to architecting AI systems serving billions at a leading tech company.

During his eight years in Silicon Valley, Mehta earned recognition as both technical genius and pragmatic problem-solver. But while peers chased stock options, he soon began seeking out projects with tangible real-world applications, finding the cycle of optimizing engagement metrics and ad revenue increasingly hollow.

Mehta embodies Silicon Valley's casual confidence, favoring jeans and plain t-shirts over formal business attire. His communication style is direct and enthusiastic, particularly when discussing technology's problem-solving potential. Despite impressive achievements, he maintains humility, and is eager to learn from others regardless of their position.

The Chief AI Officer role at ThermaDynamics represents everything he's been seeking: the application of cutting-edge technology to tangible industrial challenges. He sees potential to transform a traditional manufacturer into a technology leader, creating intelligent systems that work better and contribute to sustainability. The challenge of modernizing legacy systems and upskilling a traditional workforce energizes rather than intimidates him.

Thomas Greaves

Thomas Greaves embodies ThermaDynamics' evolution from regional player to global force in climate control systems. His journey from ambitious young engineer in 1987 to CEO mirrors the company's own transformation. Lean and angular, with silver-gray hair and sharp features giving him an air of perpetual intensity, he cuts a different figure from the traditional industrial CEO.

During his decade as CEO, sixty-three-year-old Greaves has built a reputation for bold ambition and calculated risks. His leadership combines old-school industrial wisdom with appreciation for technological innovation. He's expanded into new markets, quadrupled market capitalization, and navigated globalization challenges, while never forgetting his mentor Richard Steele's fundamental lesson: in their business, reliability is everything.

Greaves operates with the confidence of someone who's worked through every organizational level. His communication is direct and thoughtful, equally comfortable discussing technical specifications with engineers and strategic vision with the board.

Entering what may be his final career chapter, Greaves remains focused on positioning ThermaDynamics for long-term success, seeing himself not just as steward of the present, but also an architect of its future. After all, he wasn't brought in to maintain the company, but to grow it, challenge it, transform it.

Richard Steele

Richard Steele remains a commanding presence at ThermaDynamics despite time's visible toll. His forty-eight-year journey began in sales, where leadership abilities quickly marked him for advancement. As CEO from age thirty-eight, he transformed the regional player into a respected name in industrial climate control through careful expansion, strong customer relationships, and unwavering focus on product reliability.

While the Richard Steele of the early days was known for bold decisions and calculated risks, qualities he encouraged in young Thomas Greaves, time has transformed the seventy-eight year old into a more conservative figure. Where he once saw opportunities, he now sees threats; where he championed change, he counsels caution. This shift hasn't gone unnoticed by board members caught between his historically successful approach and rapidly changing market demands.

Despite officially relinquishing operational control a decade ago, Steele maintains an unusually active presence in daily operations, often walking the factory floor or offering unsolicited operational advice, sometimes creating tension with the current management team. Yet beneath this cautious exterior, glimpses of the old Steele emerge when new ideas connect to his fundamental principles. His pride in ThermaDynamics is evident in every interaction; for him, the company isn't just a business but a legacy he's dedicated his life to building and protecting.

Maria Fernandes

Maria Fernandes represents the backbone of ThermaDynamics' technological infrastructure. As Chief Information Officer for the past eight years, she's built and maintained the robust systems keeping the company running. Her approach is methodical and security-focused, shaped by two decades in traditional industrial companies before joining ThermaDynamics.

Fernandes' IT department runs like a well-oiled machine, with high service levels and strong security protocols. Her team appreciates her clear direction and unwavering support, earning their loyalty by shielding them from politics while fighting for resources. Under her leadership, core systems have remained steady and reliable, if not cutting-edge. Her challenge is maintaining stability while adapting to evolving needs.

Known for direct communication and no-nonsense approach, fifty-four-year-old Fernandes views technology through the lens of business necessity rather than innovation for innovation's sake. She takes pride in keeping systems secure, believing reliability trumps flashy features. However, this conservative approach has led some to suggest ThermaDynamics has fallen behind competitors in integrating new technologies.

The creation of a separate AI division under a new Chief AI Officer has struck a nerve with Fernandes. She believes AI is fundamentally a technology challenge dependent on the infrastructure her team manages. This decision feels like a vote of no confidence despite her years of service, creating tension that complicates the company's transformation.

Fred LaPlante

At forty-eight, Fred LaPlante embodies ThermaDynamics' operational heart. His fifteen-year rise from factory floor engineer to Chief Operating Officer has shaped the company's reputation for market-leading reliability. His French accent remains pronounced despite years in the UK, worn as proudly as his engineering credentials.

LaPlante's approach to operations is rooted in 'industrial wisdom', combining rigorous engineering principles with hard-won practical experience. Under his leadership, ThermaDynamics' manufacturing processes have become a model of consistency and quality control. He takes personal pride in industry-leading reliability statistics and low failure rates, achievements earning him significant organizational influence.

LaPlante views AI and sustainability initiatives with unconcealed skepticism, seeing expensive distractions from building reliable climate control systems. He evaluates proposed changes through the lens of operational risk, where every process modification, technology integration, or 'green' material substitution potentially threatens his hard-established quality standards.

Yet beneath his resistance lies a deeper truth: LaPlante's success building ultra-reliable products has come at innovation's expense. While ThermaDynamics' systems don't often fail, they also rarely excite. His focus on prudence and caution, while delivering consistency, has opened doors for innovative competitors to capture customers seeking next-generation solutions.

Saskia Schmidt

Saskia Schmidt is the newest addition to ThermaDynamics' leadership team, joining as Chief HR Officer just eighteen months ago. She combines analytical rigor from her consulting background with a deep understanding of organizational dynamics. Her German-Jamaican heritage and international experience provide a unique lens on corporate culture and change management.

Unlike colleagues who rose through industrial or technical ranks, Schmidt's path to ThermaDynamics went through blue-chip corporations and top-tier consulting firms. This background gives her a broader perspective on business transformation, having witnessed successes and failures across multiple industries, while demonstrating skill translating this experience into practical insights for an industrial setting.

Despite her relatively short tenure, forty-two-year-old Schmidt's influence has grown quickly. Her opinion carries significant weight in management discussions due to her ability to frame business challenges in human terms. She has an uncanny talent for reading organizational undercurrents and anticipating how changes will ripple through the workforce.

While naturally optimistic about innovation, Schmidt maintains that transformation must build on engaged employees and supportive leadership. She often reminds colleagues that 'technology may drive change, but people determine its success.' Her approach emphasizes the human side of business transformation – training, communication, and cultural alignment.

Serge Closer

The fifty-two-year-old Serge Closer represents ThermaDynamics' commercial engine. His twenty years with the company have paralleled its expansion from a UK-focused operation to a global force. As Executive Vice President of Sales, he leads a network of regional directors with the same energy and enthusiasm he brought to his first sales role.

Closer's approach is fundamentally relationship-driven. He knows the names of the key technical buyers at major customers, remembers their children's ages, and recalls specific installation challenges from years-old projects. This personal touch, combined with deep industry knowledge, has built a loyal customer base valuing his candid advice as much as the products.

Recent market pressures have changed his customer conversations. Discussions once centered on reliability and performance specs now increasingly address energy efficiency, environmental impact, and smart features. Despite his traditional background, Closer has become pragmatically open to new approaches. "Twenty years ago, customers bought our units because they worked better," he often says. "Now they're asking how our units can help them work better."

His outgoing personality and natural optimism make him popular throughout the company, comfortable sharing jokes with factory workers or presenting to the board. However, beneath his gregarious exterior lies a shrewd business operator who understands that staying relevant means embracing change, even when uncomfortable.

Katarina Svensson

Katarina Svensson brings a clear-eyed financial perspective to ThermaDynamics' leadership team. As Chief Financial Officer for the last five years, the forty-six-year-old has established herself as the voice of fiscal prudence and practical reality. Her previous experience as CFO of a Swedish industrial firm provides deep understanding of the sector's financial dynamics and investment cycles.

Svensson's approach to financial management is methodical and numbers-driven. She has little patience for proposals lacking solid business cases or relying on optimistic projections. In meetings, she's known for cutting through elaborate strategic visions with pointed questions about costs, returns, and timelines. "That sounds impressive," she will often say, "but what's the payback period?" Her attitude stems not from resistance to change, but from understanding how financial markets judge industrial companies and how thin margins become during transformation efforts.

She's developed a reputation for being tough but fair, supporting well-structured initiatives showing clear paths to profitability while challenging projects driven more by enthusiasm than economics. Her Swedish directness, combined with financial expertise, makes her formidable in investment discussions.

For Svensson, every major investment must answer three questions: How much will it cost? When will it pay back? What are the risks? While this approach sometimes puts her at odds with those pushing faster transformation, it has helped the company avoid potentially costly missteps.

14

Prologue

September 1987, Maidenhead, UK

Thomas Greaves straightened his tie for the third time as he walked through the glass doors of ThermaDynamics' headquarters. The morning sun glinted off the bronze company logo mounted on the brick façade - a stylized 'TD' with heat waves rising above it. At twenty-five, with a fresh master's degree in engineering, he felt equal parts excitement and trepidation about his first day.

The lobby hadn't changed since his interviews two months ago: the same faded industrial carpet, the cork bulletin board covered with employee notices and safety reminders, and a slight hint of machine oil in the air. What had changed was his perspective. This wasn't just another corporate office anymore; this was *his* workplace now.

"Mr. Greaves?" A secretary appeared from behind the reception desk. "Mr. Steele is ready to see you."

Greaves followed her through a maze of cubicles and workshops. The manufacturing floor hummed beyond a set of double doors, a steady rhythm of pistons and welding torches that would become the backdrop to his professional life. Engineers hunched over drafting tables, their sleeves rolled up, pencils moving with precise determination across technical drawings. A few looked up as he passed, sizing up the new arrival in his overly large suit.

Richard Steele's office was exactly what you'd expect from the CEO of a medium-sized industrial company: functional, organized, with a view of the parking lot and a second factory beyond. The man himself stood as Thomas entered - tall, broad-shouldered, with the kind of commanding presence that filled a room.

"Thomas, welcome aboard," Steele's handshake was firm, his smile genuine. At forty, he was young for a CEO, but his reputation in the industry was already substantial. "How does it feel to be joining the TD family?"

"Excited to get started, sir," Thomas replied, taking the offered seat. "I've been reading everything I could find about our product lines and market position."

Steele nodded approvingly. "Good. We're not the biggest player out there, but we're solid. Know why?" He gestured to a framed photo on his wall – a group of workers gathered around what appeared to be the company's first industrial cooling unit. "Because we understand that in this business, reliability isn't just a feature – it's everything. Our customers can't afford downtime."

He leaned forward, his expression intensifying. "But here's what keeps me up at night: the market's changing. Japanese manufacturers are getting aggressive on price. Everyone's talking about computerized controls. And our customers?" He shook his head. "They're starting to ask questions about energy efficiency that we don't have good answers for yet."

Thomas felt his pulse quicken. This wasn't just the usual first-day orientation, this was a CEO sharing his strategic concerns with a junior engineer. He chose his next words carefully. "Do you see these as threats or opportunities, Mr. Steele?"

A smile cracked across Steele's face. "Both. Always both. That's why we need young blood like you, Thomas. Fresh eyes. New perspectives." He stood and walked to the window, looking out at the factory. "You know what I see out there? Not just machines and workers. I see families that depend on us. Communities that count on us. Customers who trust us." He turned back to Thomas. "Think you're ready for that kind of responsibility?"

Thomas stood, matching Steele's gaze. "Yes, sir. I am."

"Good." Steele checked his watch. "Our head of R&D is expecting you. He'll show you around, get you started on your first project." He extended his hand again. "Welcome to ThermaDynamics, Thomas. Make us proud."

As Thomas left the office, his mind was already racing with possibilities. He couldn't have known then how that conversation would echo through the decades to come, or that one day he would be the one standing at that same window, facing challenges that would make today's concerns seem quaint by comparison.

But that was all in the future. For now, he had a first day to tackle, and somewhere nearby, the head of R&D was waiting.

ACT 1

ARRIVAL AND RESISTANCE

Chapter 1

A COMPANY AT A CROSSROADS

Transformation starts not with a strategy,
but with the courage to admit what's no longer working.

June 2025, Maidenhead, UK
Thomas Greaves stood at the same window where Richard Steele had delivered his memorable speech thirty-eight years ago. The view had changed dramatically—the old warehouse complex had been transformed into a modern campus, but the weight of responsibility felt exactly the same.
At sixty-three, Greaves cut a different figure than his predecessor. Where

Steele had commanded attention with his imposing build and broad shoulders, Greaves was slender and angular, with silver-gray hair framing sharp features that suggested a mind perpetually in motion. The Wall Street Journal had once described him as 'looking more like a tech CEO than the leader of an industrial giant' - a comparison he hadn't minded at all.

"The quarterly numbers are in, sir."

Sophia Alexiou, his Chief of Staff, appeared in the doorway with a tablet in hand. She'd been with the company for five years and had an uncanny ability to read his moods. Alexiou had always been more than just a Chief of Staff. She had a hand in everything, from market intelligence to leadership planning. If anyone could help navigate the current challenges, it was her. Today, her careful tone told him everything he needed to know about the contents of her report.

"How bad?" he asked, not turning from the window.

"Revenue down 8% year-over-year. Profit margins compressed by 3 points."

Greaves nodded slowly. The numbers weren't unexpected, but they still stung. Under his ten years of leadership, ThermaDynamics had transformed from a regional player into a global force in industrial and commercial climate control systems. The market cap, $2 billion when he took over, had quadrupled to $8 billion under his leadership, reflecting significant growth before the recent downturn. The company's climate control systems could be found in everything from factories to apartment buildings to offshore wind farms to data centers. But lately, the ground had been shifting beneath their feet.

He turned to face Alexiou. "Show me the competitor analysis."

She turned her tablet around, displaying a detailed dashboard of market share data and competitive intelligence.

"CoolTech's new AI-driven systems are eating into our commercial market share," Alexiou began. "Their predictive maintenance capabilities are..." she hesitated, searching for a diplomatic word.

"Better than ours," Greaves finished for her. "And cheaper too, I imagine."

"Yes. And on the industrial side, Zhongwei Thermal is undercutting us by 30% in Asia. Their quality isn't quite there yet, but..."

"But it will be soon enough." Greaves walked over to his desk and searched for an email. "Meanwhile, Titan Motors is the latest to push for carbon neutrality. Half of our major customers have made similar commitments for 2030 or 2035. Deutsche Bank, Singapore Airlines, the NHS, they're all reviewing their supplier sustainability credentials."

Alexiou's expression tightened. She knew what that meant. ThermaDynamics' product line, while efficient by traditional standards, wasn't designed with sustainability as a core principle. Retrofitting existing products would be expensive. Developing new ones would be even worse.

"The board of directors meeting," she prompted gently. "What's our strategy?"

Greaves smiled for the first time that morning. "Tell me, Sophia, what do you know about dual transformation?"

She blinked, caught off guard by the apparent non sequitur. "The concept from business school? Running your core business while simultaneously building the future?"

"Yes." He turned back to the window, but this time his gaze was focused on the horizon rather than the factory. "But this isn't your typical dual transformation, Sophia. I've been thinking a lot about the megatrends that will shape our industry's future. Not just the obvious ones - demographics, urbanization, globalization - but the ones that will fundamentally transform how we operate. And two stand out above all others: artificial intelligence and sustainability." He paused, letting that sink in. "Everyone's talking about AI. Everyone's talking about sustainability. But who's thinking about how they work together? Who's considering how they might transform an industry that hasn't fundamentally changed in decades?"

Alexiou was making notes on her tablet. "You want to pursue both simultaneously? The investment required would be..."

"Substantial," he acknowledged. "And risky. The board won't like it. Richard will probably have a fit." He chuckled, thinking of his former mentor, now chairman of the board. "But you know what's riskier? Doing nothing. Watching while tech companies eat our lunch on one side and Asian manufacturers undercut us on the other. This isn't a dual transformation in the business school sense. It's a twin transformation."

A reminder popped up on Alexiou's tablet - sixty minutes until the board meeting. She raised an eyebrow questioningly.

"Give me thirty minutes to review my presentation," Greaves said, his hand instinctively moving to straighten a tie that was no longer there, a gesture that momentarily transported him back to his first day. "It's time to choose a path."

As Alexiou left the office, Greaves reflected on the conversation he'd had in this office all those years ago. The challenges were different now: Instead of computerized controls, they were facing artificial intelligence; instead of basic energy efficiency, they were grappling with full-scale sustainability transformation. He knew the board would push back. Steele, and many of the others would see threats before opportunities. But if they hesitated now, there might not be another chance.

Both, he thought. Always both.

Chapter 2

A BOARD MANDATE FOR A TWIN TRANSFORMATION

The hardest part isn't getting approval,
it's making them believe in what they can't yet see.

A Strategic Proposal

The ThermaDynamics boardroom hadn't changed much in the past decade. The same mahogany table dominated the space, though the leather chairs were new and the far wall now housed a large display screen instead of the old whiteboard. What had changed was the tension in the air.

Richard Steele sat at the head of the table, his once-dark hair now mostly gone, his frame having acquired a substantial paunch over the decades. But at seventy-eight, after forty-eight years with the company, his presence remained as commanding as ever, filling the room just as it had done in his CEO days. The other board members, eleven in total, were arranged around the table, their expressions ranging from concerned to skeptical. The quarterly numbers displayed on their tablets had set a somber tone for the meeting.

"Before we move to the main agenda," Steele began, his voice carrying its familiar gravitas, "I believe Thomas has a strategic proposal to present."

Greaves stood, aware of all eyes in the room turning to him. He'd spent the last few days refining his presentation, but looking at the faces around the table, he knew this would be more about conviction than slides.

"Ladies and gentlemen," Greaves cleared his voice and began, "we're at an inflection point. The numbers you've seen today aren't just a temporary dip, they're a warning sign. Our industry is changing faster than at any point in our history."

He clicked to the first slide, showing the competitive landscape. "CoolTech's AI systems are capturing our premium customers. Zhongwei Thermal is eating into our market share with aggressive pricing. And…" he paused, making eye contact with each board member. "…many of our customers are demanding sustainability credentials we don't have."

"We've faced challenges before," interrupted James Morrison, one of the longest-serving board members. "We've always adapted. Made incremental improvements."

"Incremental won't cut it this time," Greaves countered. "We need transformation. But not just any transformation." He clicked to the next slide, which showed two intersecting circles labeled 'AI' and 'Sustainability'. "We need to pursue both artificial intelligence and sustainability, not as separate initiatives, but as an integrated strategy, what I'm calling a 'Twin Transformation'."

Patricia Wong, who had joined the board two years ago from a major tech company, leaned forward. "I get the need to focus on AI. The future is data, connectivity, and digital. But, sustainability as well? To go for both? Isn't that a bit… ambitious?"

"More than ambitious; it's reckless," cut in Morrison. "The costs alone…"

"The costs will be substantial," Greaves acknowledged. "But the cost of doing nothing would be far greater." He clicked to a slide showing projected market share decline. "This is where we're headed if we don't act. And this…" he switched to the next slide, "is what our competitors are already doing."

The room fell silent as the board members studied the data. Steele's expression was unreadable, his fingers drumming softly on the table.

"Let's be concrete. What exactly are you proposing, Thomas?" he asked finally.

"Two new C-level positions," Greaves replied. "A Chief Sustainability Officer and a Chief AI Officer, both reporting directly to me. A dedicated budget for the transformation. And most importantly, a mandate to integrate or 'twin' these initiatives across every aspect of our business."

James Morrison hunched closer, frowning.

"I understand the need for an AI leader, but why centralize sustainability under a single executive? Sustainability should be embedded in every department. Each leader should manage their own budget instead of handing it over to a CSO."

A few board members nodded in agreement. For years, sustainability budgets had been spread across operations, R&D, marketing, finance, and supply chain, with each department handling its own initiatives independently. Now, Greaves was proposing to centralize the entire sustainability budget under the CSO's control.

Greaves folded his hands and let the room settle before responding.

"That's the same argument people used to make about finance," he said evenly. "Every department should be able to manage its budget in a meaningful and reliable way. And they do. But there's a reason we have a CFO."

He let the words hang for a moment.

"The CFO doesn't take away financial responsibility from department heads, but someone has to oversee the numbers, ensure alignment with strategy, and allocate resources where they have the highest impact. Otherwise, you end up with disconnected efforts, inefficiencies, and no clear accountability."

He tapped the document on the table in front of him.

"Sustainability's no different. We don't just need projects scattered across departments. We need a clear strategy, a unified budget, and a leader who can drive execution at scale. That's why we need a CSO."

Richard Steele exhaled sharply.

"Fine. But this had better generate value, not just reports."

Greaves gave a small nod.

"The shareholders won't like it," Morrison warned. "Not with these quarterly numbers. Two new expensive executives…"

"The shareholders will like bankruptcy even less," Wong interjected. "I've seen this pattern before in tech. When disruption hits, it hits fast."

"I'd like to know how this will impact jobs?" Olly Ramsdale, the Board's employee representative, spoke up for the first time. "You know what people will think about when they hear 'AI'."

"Should this really be our priority, with these results?" exclaimed Roger Mann, a retired banker and close friend of Steele.

Steele raised a hand, silencing the growing debate. "Thomas, you've been CEO for ten years. It's been a good ride and you've earned the right to be heard. But this..." he gestured at the slides, "this twin thing, it's a big bet. Perhaps the biggest in our company's history."

"It is," Greaves agreed. "But remember what you told me on my first day? About threats and opportunities?"

A flicker of recognition crossed Steele's face. "Yes. Yes. Both. Always both."

"Exactly. These challenges - AI and sustainability - they're not just threats. They're opportunities to reinvent ourselves. To lead rather than follow." Greaves straightened his shoulders. "But we need to act now, while we still have the resources and market position to make it work."

A murmur of conversation spread around the boardroom. While doubts lingered on some faces, it was clear that not everyone was opposed to the plan. In fact, most of the board seemed receptive, at least to part of it.

"For me, the AI transformation makes sense," said Wong, tapping her pen against the table. "Market intelligence is showing a clear trend: Companies that don't integrate AI into their operations now will be outpaced within a decade. Predictive maintenance, IoT, smart automation, demand forecasting... these are obvious business imperatives."

James Morrison nodded.

"I won't argue that AI is the future. And from an operational standpoint, it can improve efficiency and cost control in ways we desperately need right now."

Others around the table murmured their agreement. Support for the AI component of the strategy didn't seem to be an issue.

"But sustainability?" Morrison leaned back, shaking his head. "That's where you lose me. It sounds great on paper, but at the end of the day, it's a compliance headache. I want to save the planet as much as the next man, but, let's face it... it's going to be a costly distraction from our core business."

A few more board members nodded. "We're an industrial company," another member added. "Our customers care about reliability, price, and efficiency. Carbon footprint is, well, to be honest, it's a 'nice to have'."

Richard Steele, who had remained uncharacteristically quiet until now, spoke. "I'm not against sustainability, Thomas. But let's be realistic, how many of our customers are truly making buying decisions based on ESG scores? AI is fast becoming a competitive necessity. But sustainability?" He shrugged. "I need to see how it ties back to the bottom line before I can get behind it."

Greaves had expected this pushback. He had spent enough years in boardrooms to know that sustainability, framed as an ethical imperative, would never win over a room full of hard-nosed business leaders. But framed correctly - as a business strategy - it could.

He let the skepticism settle for a moment. Then he spoke, his voice calm but resolute.

"Sustainability is not the goal," he said, scanning the room. "Competitiveness is. Profitability is. Sustainability just happens to be a byproduct of doing business the right way."

A few board members frowned, uncertain. One openly rolled his eyes.

"Let me put it another way," Greaves continued. "When we improve energy efficiency, we lower costs. When we make our supply chain more resilient, we reduce risk. When we reduce material waste, we improve margins. And when we anticipate regulatory shifts before they happen, we avoid costly compliance penalties. Every move we make to improve efficiency, flexibility, and resilience naturally makes us more sustainable as well as more competitive."

He gestured toward the analysis on the screen. "And if we don't do it? Someone else will. The companies that survive the next decade won't be the ones that check ESG boxes for show. They'll be the ones that build smarter, leaner, more adaptable businesses. And guess what? Those businesses will also have the best sustainability scores."

Steele studied him, tapping his fingers on the table.

"So, you're saying we don't chase sustainability for its own sake. We chase performance. And sustainability follows."

"Exactly," Greaves confirmed. "We're going to put the AI in sustainable. But not because we're going green. Because we're going smart. That's why it's a twin transformation."

The murmur of doubt had quieted. No one was applauding, but Greaves could see the shift in their expressions. The argument had landed. As he sat down, Steele called for a vote.

"The proposal passes," he announced after counting the raised hands, "but not unanimously." He fixed Greaves with a stern look. "You've got your mandate, Thomas. Don't make us regret it."

At the end of the meeting, while board members filed out, Steele and Greaves remained seated, with Steele looking thoughtful. "Two new C-level positions," he mused. "That's going to shake things up."

"They need shaking up," Greaves replied.

"Yes," Steele agreed. "But not everyone will thank you for it." He stood slowly, gathering his papers. "The hard part starts now, Thomas. Leading change is one thing. Leading transformation?" He shook his head. "That's something else entirely."

Leaving the boardroom, Greaves felt the weight of what he'd just set in motion. The twin transformation would change everything - processes, products, people. Some would embrace it. Others would resist. But there was no turning back now.

His phone buzzed with a message from Chief of Staff Alexiou: "HR's ready to start the search for the new positions. When do we announce?"

"Tomorrow," he typed back. "Time to shake things up."

Chapter 3

NEW HIRES

They spoke different languages,
but were being asked to write the same future.

A Clash of Worlds

Six months later, Elena Navarro found herself checking her watch in the executive waiting room at ThermaDynamics' headquarters. It was her first day on the job, and she was ten minutes early for her first official meeting with Greaves. She smoothed her charcoal suit and glanced up as a casually dressed middle-aged man entered the room.

He extended his hand. "Vikram Mehta. Digital Transformation and AI."

"Elena Navarro," she replied, her grip firm. "Sustainability."

Recognition flashed in his eyes. "Ah, the other newbie! I've been wanting to meet you."

Navarro was about to answer, but before she could so do, a raised voice cut through the door of the CEO's office.

"You're gambling the company's future on unproven concepts," said a gravelly voice.

"The board approved this direction, Richard," another voice responded firmly. "We can't keep doing what we've always done and expect different results."

"The board approved a reasonable exploration, not this... crusade you're embarking on. Shareholders are asking questions I don't have answers to."

"These are the experts we need to navigate what's coming. You know as well as I do that our industry is changing."

"What I know is that revenue is down close to double digits, and instead of focusing on our core business, you're chasing trends."

Sitting outside the room, Navarro and Mehta exchanged uncomfortable glances. At the nearby desk, an executive assistant suddenly became intensely focused on her computer screen, fingers typing with unnecessary

vigour as the voices grew louder.

"They're not trends, they're the future. Give me time to prove it."

"Time is a luxury we don't have," the gravelly voice objected.

The door suddenly swung open. Richard Steele emerged, taking in the waiting room with a quick sweep of his eyes, his expression hardening when he spotted Navarro and Mehta. He paused, studying them both with piercing blue eyes.

"You must be the new transformation experts," he said, his tone polite, but not without an edge.

"Artificial intelligence and digital transformation," Mehta said, standing up.

"Sustainability and environmental innovation," Navarro added, maintaining eye contact.

"Ah," said Steele, "one for computers, one for trees. Welcome to ThermaDynamics. I hope you both understand what you've signed up for." He glanced back toward Greaves's office. "Thomas has great faith in you, and I support him." He stepped closer, lowering his voice. "But a word of advice: in this company, results speak louder than words. And we need those results sooner rather than later."

With that, he strode past them, leaving an awkward silence in his wake.

Thomas Greaves was now standing in the doorway to his office, his expression briefly revealing the tension of the previous conversation before breaking into a welcoming smile.

"Elena, Vikram, please come in," he said, gesturing them inside. "I see you've met our Chairman."

Ever the pragmatist, Greaves wasted no time with pleasantries. He motioned for them to take seats across from his desk, then sat down himself and leaned forward with a serious look on his face. "You're both here because we need to do something extraordinary," he began. "Elena, your job is to make us the greenest manufacturing company in our sector. Vikram, you're here to make our products smarter and our systems more efficient."

He paused, his eyes narrowing. "But let me be absolutely clear about something. This isn't about saving the planet or pursuing technological novelty for its own sake. This is about securing ThermaDynamics' future in a rapidly changing marketplace."

Greaves stood and walked to the window, gesturing at the sprawling manufacturing campus below. "Our competitors are either undercutting our prices or outpacing our innovation. We need tangible, measurable business results, like increased efficiency, reduced costs, new revenue streams, and clear market differentiation."

He turned back to face them. "The board didn't approve your positions because they suddenly developed environmental consciousness or technological curiosity. They approved them because they believe - or at least I've convinced them to believe - that sustainability and AI are the keys to our continued profitability. This isn't about doing the right things. It's about doing the smart things for our business."

Returning to his seat, Greaves continued, "So, when you develop your strategies and initiatives, every single one needs to have a clear business case. If you can't explain how it improves our bottom line, it won't get funded. You heard the Chairman, and I can tell you he's not alone. Is that understood?"

Both Mehta and Navarro nodded.

"And another thing. I don't want you to work in silos. The future of this company depends on the two of you finding ways to combine and amplify your impact."

As he spoke, Greaves slid a document across the desk outlining ThermaDynamics' Twin Transformation strategy - a plan that required significant investment, bold decision-making, and seamless collaboration between sustainability and AI-driven digital transformation. The board had approved the plan, but execution was another matter entirely.

Greaves let out a sharp breath, as he flipped the page to reveal a spreadsheet. "Here's what makes it even harder."

They both scanned the numbers. Revenue was down. Profits had slipped. The share price had taken a hit. ThermaDynamics had increased its dividend slightly to maintain investor confidence, but that was a short-term fix. Worse, a new line of commercial air conditioning units had developed quality issues, leading to increased warranty claims and a growing number of dissatisfied customers.

"We're under pressure," Greaves admitted. "Not just from the market, but from inside this company. There will be resistance. Many executives think this transformation is a distraction. Others think it's a waste of money. And if we don't prove them wrong, the board might start pulling back support. I'll support you as long as I can, but it won't be forever."

Mehta's brow furrowed. He had expected challenges, but financial pressure and internal resistance on day one? That raised the stakes considerably.

Navarro, however, met Greaves' gaze head-on. "Then we'll launch sustainability and AI initiatives, and prove that they drive performance. If we do this, the skeptics will have no choice but to get on board."

Greaves allowed himself the faintest hint of a smile. "That's the mindset we need."

He stood, signaling the meeting's end. "You'd better get to work. You'll need each other more than you realize."

As they left the office, Mehta turned to Navarro with a concerned look in his eyes. "Looks like we're in for a fight."

Navarro smiled, evidently unfazed. "Then we'd better make sure we win."

Mehta looked at his phone, "It's ten o'clock now, how about we meet for lunch and start planning our next moves."

"Great," Navarro replied, "the cafeteria at noon?"

The Pragmatic Environmentalist

Navarro's heels clicked purposefully down the corridor as she made her way back to her newly assigned office. The meeting with Greaves had been illuminating, and sobering. The magnitude of the task settled on her shoulders like a heavy cloak.

The office they'd given her overlooked the manufacturing facility, a constant reminder of the challenge ahead. Elena set her leather portfolio on the desk and gazed out at the smokestacks in the distance. It was a view that would have horrified her younger self, the idealistic graduate who had once chained herself to trees to prevent logging.

That seemed like another lifetime now. Her journey from environmental activist to corporate sustainability leader had been anything but linear. A decade at an NGO had taken her from the muddy banks of the Amazon to the pristine conference rooms of the United Nations. She'd waded through toxic waste in industrial zones and negotiated with corporate executives who could barely conceal their disdain for what they viewed as environmental theatrics.

As Navarro sat down in her chair, her fingers running along the edge of the desk, her mind briefly drifted to her childhood in Galicia, in the industrial, rain-soaked northwest of Spain. Far from the sun-drenched tourist havens of the Costa Blanca, she had grown up in the shadow of factories and shipyards, where the Atlantic winds carried both the salt of the sea and the acrid scents of industry. Her hometown of Ferrol had been defined by its massive shipbuilding complex - a place where environmental concerns took a distant backseat to economic survival.

She had witnessed firsthand how the decline of those industries had devastated her community, leaving behind unemployment and environmental scars in equal measure. That experience had shaped her understanding of sustainability in ways that some of her more privileged university classmates, with their abstract ideals, could never fully comprehend. For Navarro, environmental progress couldn't come at the expense of livelihoods; it had to work in concert with economic reality.

That was what had made her effective at all the jobs she had; not just her passion, though she had that in abundance, but her pragmatism. While others shouted slogans, she built spreadsheets. While activists demanded immediate cessation of harmful practices, she crafted five-year transition plans that corporations could actually implement.

She picked up the framed photo she'd brought, the only personal item she'd unpacked so far. It showed her standing beside the CEO of a chemical company, both smiling as they cut the ribbon on a new zero-emissions processing plant. That project had reduced the company's carbon footprint by 30% while increasing operational efficiency by 15%. The numbers had spoken for themselves. She'd done it before, and now she'd have to do it again.

Numbers, Navarro knew, would be her most powerful tool at ThermaDynamics. When Greaves had first approached her, her instinct had been to decline. The company's reputation wasn't terrible, but it wasn't exemplary either. It was middle of the pack in environmental ratings, with half-hearted sustainability initiatives that felt more like marketing than commitment.

But then she'd seen the potential. ThermaDynamics' products were in millions of homes and businesses worldwide. Even incremental improvements in energy efficiency or materials would cascade into massive environmental benefits at scale. The challenge Greaves presented in the document he had shared - cutting carbon emissions by 50% in five years while improving the bottom line - was exactly the kind of seemingly impossible task she was excited to solve.

She logged in to her new laptop and pulled up the organizational chart. Her newly inherited sustainability team was previously divided into two distinct groups. One part had been embedded in R&D, where they focused on materials innovation and product design. The other part came from finance, where they handled sustainability reporting and regulatory compliance. These two groups had never functioned as a unified team with a coherent strategy; they barely even spoke the same language. The team's composition was equally fragmented: several members were company veterans with decades of experience, while others were recent hires, mostly brought on to address new regulatory requirements. Unifying them would be her first challenge.

And then there was Mehta, the AI expert whose path would inevitably intersect with hers. She had researched him thoroughly. His work at one of the digital giants had revolutionized their production processes, but there was no indication he'd ever considered sustainability as a factor in his work.

She leaned back in her chair, contemplating the monumental task ahead. This wasn't about saving the world - Greaves had made that abundantly clear. This was about saving and transforming a company. But if she succeeded, she might just do both.

Navarro glanced at her phone, resisting the urge to check for messages from her children. Both were attending university in Madrid, Lucia studying architecture, Miguel pursuing engineering. They were adjusting well to their parents' recent divorce, finalized just three months ago after years of growing apart. It had been amicable but exhausting. In many ways, ThermaDynamics had offered the perfect escape: a new challenge in a new country, an opportunity to redefine herself professionally while establishing a fresh personal beginning. She was free from the roles and routines that had come to feel like comfortable but restrictive boundaries in Spain. The thought was both terrifying and exhilarating.

The intercom buzzed, interrupting her thoughts. Her new assistant informed her that her team was assembled in the conference room, waiting to meet their new leader.

Elena closed her laptop and stood. Time to begin.

The Idealistic Architect

Vikram Mehta stood at the window of his new office, hands clasped behind his back, gazing out at the sprawling ThermaDynamics campus. The contrast to his previous workplace, a sleek, open-concept tech hub in Palo Alto, couldn't have been starker. Here, industrial pragmatism has replaced Silicon Valley utopianism.

He moved to his desk and tapped a fist on the polished mahogany, a tangible reminder of the company's decades-long traditions. As he settled into his chair, Mehta allowed himself a moment to reflect on the journey that had brought him here.

Born in Bangalore during India's emergence as a global tech powerhouse, Mehta had been coding games since he was ten, dismantling computers by twelve, and building rudimentary neural networks by sixteen. His parents, his father a mathematics teacher, his mother a systems engineer, had nurtured his technical curiosity but also instilled in him a sense that technology should serve humanity, not the other way around.

With a combination of smarts and a solid work ethic, he made it first into IIT, and then Stanford, before landing a job at one of the tech giants. There, he had architected AI systems and created algorithms that could predict user behavior with uncanny accuracy. His work had earned him professional accolades along with the financial security that his immigrant parents had dreamed for him.

Yet, three years into his role as VP, a hollow feeling had started to creep in. During a particularly grueling product launch, the realization hit him: he had spent six months perfecting an algorithm whose sole purpose was to keep users watching videos for 2.3 minutes longer. Was this really what he wanted his legacy to be?

The same week he updated his LinkedIn profile for the first time in years.

ThermaDynamics' offer had come as a surprise - a traditional manufacturing company seeking an AI innovator. The initial conversations with Greaves had been electrifying. Here was a CEO who understood that the future belonged not to those who simply built better hardware, but to those who created intelligent systems that could learn, adapt, and optimize in real-time.

The location had been another powerful draw. While Silicon Valley had been his professional home for years, the opportunity to relocate to the UK had resonated on a deeply personal level. Many of his extended family had settled in Britain after leaving India, creating a network that had always felt tantalizingly close yet just out of reach during his years in California. The thought of his two children - Arjun, eight, and Priya, six - growing up with cousins nearby, absorbing cultural traditions firsthand rather than through occasional video calls, had factored significantly into his decision. After years of building digital connections, Mehta was eager to strengthen the human ones that connected his children to their roots.

Like Navarro, Mehta was coming to terms with his new organization. From what he could ascertain, the company's digital and AI capabilities were scattered throughout the company. A machine learning team in IT was developing predictive maintenance algorithms that the operations technology group knew nothing about. The R&D department had IoT prototypes that weren't integrated with the company's cloud infrastructure. The customer experience team was sitting on terabytes of product usage data that nobody was analyzing.

He would have to bring together this disparate collection of traditional IT specialists, operations technology engineers, and a handful of data scientists. Uniting them would be challenging enough. But his partnership with Navarro added another layer of complexity. Mehta had never considered environmental impact as a primary design constraint in his AI systems. Energy efficiency, yes, but even that was ranked lower in importance than many other factors. Now, he would need to think bigger, to consider sustainability not as a side effect but as a core requirement.

Mehta gathered his notes. The challenge ahead was exactly what he had been looking for: A chance to apply cutting-edge technology to meaningful problems, to transform not just a company but potentially an entire industry. After years of optimizing clicks, he was finally going to build something that mattered.

A Shared Mission, But a Difficult Road Ahead

Navarro and Mehta's first lunch was pleasant. They shared small talk about their background and families. As newcomers to the UK, they had many similar experiences adapting to the culture and, of course, the weather. In subsequent meetings, however, they got down to business. Despite their shared sense of urgency, these first working sessions were riddled with friction. Their different professional languages alone made collaboration difficult. Navarro spoke in terms of climate impact, ESG compliance, and carbon accounting, while Mehta focused on data modeling, predictive analytics, and digital scaling. Conversations often became translation exercises, with both struggling to bridge their fields' differing methodologies.

Beyond language, their work styles also clashed. Navarro, accustomed to structured sustainability frameworks and long-term environmental policies, found Mehta's rapid, iterative approach chaotic and reckless. Meanwhile, Mehta saw Navarro's methodical, compliance-driven strategy as frustratingly slow and bureaucratic.

"Regulations are shifting," Navarro insisted in one of their early debates. "We have to ensure we align with EU carbon caps and global ESG reporting."

Mehta shook his head. "If we get stuck chasing compliance updates, we'll never innovate fast enough. AI can't be built around regulatory lag - it has to push ahead of it."

The disagreement wasn't just theoretical, it affected their ability to prioritize. Navarro wanted immediate alignment with government regulations and sustainability standards, while Mehta focused on building scalable AI models first, assuming compliance could be optimized later. The tension between them grew, making even the smallest strategic decisions difficult to finalize.

Yet, through their frustrations, one thing became clear: neither of them could succeed without the other. And that realization, challenging as it was, would be the key to overcoming their differences.

Chapter 4

A FRAGMENTED LANDSCAPE

You can't build a future on disconnected efforts.

Breaking Down the Silos

In their first week, Mehta and Navarro conducted a full internal audit of all AI and sustainability initiatives. What they found was staggering: there were dozens and dozens of projects, completely fragmented. Overlapping efforts wasted resources, and large gaps remained in areas that could deliver the most impact. The digital division had focused on automation and operational efficiency, while the sustainability team had been driving carbon reduction, regulatory compliance, and eco-friendly material sourcing. Despite the natural intersections of their work, there was little to no collaboration, which meant that even well-intended efforts were failing to scale.

To begin to address this fragmentation, Mehta and Navarro co-located their teams on the same floor, bringing engineers, data scientists, and sustainability experts together to facilitate collaboration and break down barriers.

One day, a couple of weeks after they had started working together, Mehta and Navarro received a message from CEO Greaves: 'Meeting with Steele tomorrow morning. Update me on progress asap.'

Navarro set her tablet down and frowned. "It's beginning already."

"What is?" Mehta asked.

"Steele and the board are nervous. If we don't show progress, the pressure is going to rise even more."

There was other news as well. Cooltech had just announced an AI-powered sustainability platform, promising 'fully optimized building management systems with built-in ESG compliance.'

Mehta scanned the report, then looked up at Navarro. "This changes things. On the downside, if they're pitching end-to-end sustainability solutions before we even have a strategy, we're a long way behind."

"What's the upside?" asked Navarro.

"Well," said Mehta, "If Cooltech is investing in AI and sustainability, it means there's something to it, and we're on the right track. It may also help the board get on board."

Navarro tapped her fingers against the table. "We need to move fast. And that means we have to fix our internal mess at the same time."

Mehta and Navarro looked over the audit findings. They highlighted several inefficiencies:

- Sustainability initiatives lacked the technological tools to effectively measure progress, with over 60% of projects relying on manual data collection and outdated spreadsheets.
- AI projects were being developed without considering any long-term environmental impact, potentially leading to efficiency gains that still contributed to excessive resource consumption.
- Both teams viewed each other with suspicion, with 70% of surveyed employees believing that the other department did not understand their priorities.
- Lack of structured communication channels had led to duplicated efforts, with both teams unknowingly working on similar projects but using different methodologies. These communication gaps were not only between the digital and sustainability teams. The audit had uncovered many overlapping projects in separate business units, functions, and markets.
- Inefficient energy use accounted for $78 million in annual waste.
- Factory automation inefficiencies were driving up production costs by 8%, leading to $250 million in excess expenditures over the past three years.

- Supply chain inefficiencies, including over-reliance on high-cost suppliers, costing $35 million annually.
- Redundant digital infrastructure and lack of cloud integration resulted in an estimated $15 million in unnecessary expenditures.

Recognizing that continuing in this disjointed manner was futile, Mehta and Navarro agreed on an urgent course of action. They would set up a task force to review the entire portfolio and establish joint governance between their teams. Their goal was to not only align their efforts but also create a structure where AI and sustainability worked in tandem rather than in parallel.

The Innovation Task Force Proposal
Determined to dismantle the silos, at least between their units, Mehta and Navarro drafted a proposal for a new governance structure. Their vision was to create an Innovation Task Force: a cross-disciplinary team composed of AI engineers, sustainability experts, operations leaders, and select representatives from finance and sales. The goal was to embed sustainability into AI-driven projects and, conversely, integrate AI capabilities into sustainability initiatives.

The Innovation Task Force would:
- Review all major digital and sustainability initiatives to ensure alignment, targeting an annual reduction of 10% in energy waste and a 15% increase in sustainable procurement compliance.
- Identify joint projects that could drive both efficiency and carbon reduction, with an initial target of cutting 30,000 metric tons of CO_2 emissions annually through a pilot project optimizing automation at a selected factory.
- Establish clear KPIs to track the financial, technological, and environmental impact of their efforts, such as reducing supply chain inefficiencies by 12% within the first year.
- Create a structured workflow that mandated early collaboration between the two teams, with a goal of increasing efficiency-related AI adoption by 25% within two years.

- Leverage AI-driven predictive analytics to assess factory energy consumption, targeting a 20% reduction in peak-hour electricity demand.
- Develop sustainability-focused AI models that optimize raw material usage, aiming for a 30% reduction in industrial waste.

To push the project forward, they also established a joint innovation lab, a dedicated space where AI engineers and sustainability teams could co-develop solutions that met both technological and environmental impact goals. This lab would serve as an incubator for new ideas, piloting cutting-edge AI-driven sustainability solutions before company-wide rollouts.

Realizing the magnitude of their task, Navarro and Mehta agreed they couldn't rely solely on internal ideas. Navarro proposed launching an open innovation initiative from the outset: "Let's create a platform inviting external innovators, researchers, and even customers to contribute ideas. This way, we quickly harness collective intelligence beyond our walls." They moved quickly to integrate this open innovation concept into their innovation lab proposal.

Mehta nodded enthusiastically.

"It'll signal to everyone, inside and outside, that we're serious about collaboration and transparency. Plus, external validation might help overcome some internal resistance."

At that stage, Navarro and Mehta's teams formed an uneasy alliance, a divided front grappling with mismatched goals, different professional languages, and clashing priorities. Progress came slowly and painfully, each small win often obscured by a tangle of misunderstandings. Conversations often felt like skirmishes, their different worldviews clashing like steel on stone. They were fighting on the same side, at least on paper, but too often it felt like a tug-of-war rather than a march toward a common goal.

Chapter 5

RESISTANCE FROM WITHIN

Every transformation is first a test of loyalty,
then of imagination.

The First Executive Leadership Team Meeting

Elena Navarro and Vikram Mehta arrived ten minutes early to the executive conference room, strategically selecting seats directly across from Thomas Greaves. Both had anticipated some resistance, but neither was prepared for the wall of hostility that awaited them.

The mahogany-paneled boardroom felt unusually cold that morning. Framed accolades and photographs of industrial facilities lined the walls, monuments to ThermaDynamics' storied past. As they filed in, chatting to one another, Navarro noticed how the executives unconsciously arranged themselves clustering at one end of the table, leaving her and Mehta isolated at the other.

When Greaves strode in, the conversation died. He introduced the newcomers with practiced corporate optimism, emphasizing the board's overwhelming approval of their twin transformation initiative. The lie hung in the air; everyone knew Chairman Steele wasn't fully committed.

"Elena and Vikram represent our future," Greaves concluded, nodding toward them. "I expect every one of you to give them your full support."

The silence that followed felt manufactured, deliberate. Fred LaPlante, the Chief Operating Officer, broke it with a dry cough.

"I'd like to understand," he said in a heavy French accent, his voice deceptively calm, "exactly how this... transformation... will impact factory throughput in the next quarter?"

LaPlante didn't wait for an answer. "Because we're already behind on production targets for the Saudi project, and I don't need more disruptions."

Mehta leaned forward. "Actually, Fred, our preliminary models show AI integration could improve throughput by fourteen percent within six months."

"Models," LaPlante interrupted, the word dripping with disdain. "Let me be honest with you. I've seen consultants come and go with their models and promises." His eyes narrowed. "What I haven't seen is AI fixing a broken assembly line at 3 AM when we're facing a deadline."

Greaves intervened. "Fred, we've discussed this. We're not just chasing trends, we're leading an inevitable shift in our industry. AI and sustainability are the future of manufacturing, whether we embrace it or not."

"The world is always changing," LaPlante shot back, color rising in his face. "What doesn't change is that we make heating and cooling systems. We make them well. We deliver them on time. Everything else is a distraction."

Maria Fernandes, the CIO, had been silently fuming. Now she spoke up.

"Since we're being direct," she said, turning to face Mehta, "I need to address the elephant in the room. AI is technology infrastructure and that is my domain." Her manicured finger tapped the table with each syllable. "We mustn't create a shadow IT department."

Mehta maintained his composure, though Navarro noticed his jaw tightening. "Maria, this isn't about territory. AI needs to be embedded everywhere."

"Precisely my point," Fernandes cut in. "And who maintains these embedded systems? Who troubleshoots them when they fail? Who ensures they meet our security protocols?" Her voice rose. "My team. My people."

The tension in the room was palpable now. Katarina Svensson, the CFO, hadn't spoken yet, but her energetic note-taking spoke volumes.

"Let's talk numbers," she finally said, not looking up from her tablet. "Our stock is down twelve percent. Commercial air conditioning units are being returned with control system failures. Sorry, Fred, but it's true. And now you want," she glanced at a document, "thirty-eight million for initial AI implementation and sustainability retrofitting."

She looked up, her gaze clinical. "Show me the ROI. Not projections or forecasts or pretty graphs. Hard numbers. When will this pay for itself?"

Navarro stepped in. "Katarina, sustainability isn't just about ROI. It's about future-proofing."

"Everything is about ROI," Svensson countered. "Especially initiatives that cost thirty-eight million during a downturn."

Navarro knew that financial discipline was a priority, but she also knew that failing to act would be far more costly in the long run. "The market is shifting. Regulations are tightening, energy prices are unpredictable, and customers are demanding sustainable solutions. If we don't invest now, we'll be scrambling to catch up later."

She leaned across the table, her voice steady. "It's not just optics anymore. Banks are recalibrating risk. Companies with strong sustainability profiles are seen as safer bets: lower environmental and regulatory risks mean lower financing costs. Some lenders now offer sustainability-linked loans: hit targets like emissions cuts, and we unlock lower interest rates. It's simple, better sustainability performance gets us cheaper capital. If we want to fund the next phase without high costs, we need to improve fast."

Navarro continued, "For years, businesses chased ratings over real resilience. Sustainability was about appearance, not long-term value. Now, investors are putting money where outcomes matter: clean energy, supply chain efficiency, advanced manufacturing, and emissions reduction. It's not about looking good. It's economic logic. Done right, sustainability goes beyond compliance, it drives resilience, innovation, and growth."

Serge Closer, Head of Sales, had been scrolling through his phone, apparently disinterested. Now he looked up with a tight smile. "Here's my reality. I have customers threatening to walk because we don't have the latest tech. I have competitors undercutting us by fifteen percent. I get the need to focus on AI, but not one client, not one, has asked about our carbon footprint this quarter."

Mehta leaned back and exhaled. "What pays the bills is staying competitive. Our competitors are already moving. CoolTech just secured a multi-year contract for AI-powered energy optimization. That could've been us."

Closer spread his hands. "Sure, let's talk about the future while we're losing the present."

The ambush was coordinated, Navarro realized. They'd prepared their arguments, decided their angles of attack. What had seemed like routine skepticism was actually organized opposition. Sensing the tension rising, she shifted the conversation. "We're not asking for blind commitment. We're asking for cooperation."

"If I may," said a quiet voice from the corner. Saskia Schmidt, the Head of HR, rarely spoke in executive meetings unless directly addressed. "We're missing something fundamental here."

All eyes turned to her.

"This isn't just about technology or sustainability as abstract concepts. It's about people. Our people." She looked directly at LaPlante. "Fred, your team is losing talent to CoolTech because they offer modern tools and purpose-driven work. Maria, your IT department has the highest turnover in the company because our best engineers want to work with cutting-edge technology."

Schmidt's gaze swept the room. "We can debate ROI and territorial boundaries all day, but while we argue, our competitors are moving forward quickly. And our best people are leaving to join them."

Her words landed like stones in still water. For a moment, no one spoke.

Then Greaves stood as if to signal an end to the meeting. "This discussion is valuable, but we're not reversing course. The board has approved this initiative, and we're moving forward." His tone left no room for further argument. "Elena, Vikram, you have three months to show preliminary results. Everyone else, you can either help shape this transformation or be shaped by it. Your choice."

As the executives filed out, the silence was thick with unspoken threats. Navarro and Mehta remained seated, stunned by the intensity of the resistance. They'd expected skepticism, not warfare.

Greaves returned after walking the others out. His expression was grim. "That," he said quietly, "was the easy part."

Mehta looked up sharply. "The easy part?"

"They were just testing boundaries. Now they'll start actively undermining you." Greaves smiled tightly. "Welcome to the executive leadership at ThermaDynamics."

As he made his way out of the boardroom, Greaves paused at the doorway, turning back as if something important had just occurred to him.

"One more thing," he said pensively. "Throughout this transformation, transparency will be critical, not only with the board but internally, among ourselves. I'd like regular updates from you both. At different points, once you've had the chance to reflect and assess your progress, send me a candid memo highlighting what's working, what's not, and the lessons you're learning along the way. These insights will be essential as we navigate forward."

Navarro and Mehta exchanged a brief, understanding glance.

"We'll make sure you're regularly updated," Navarro assured him.

"Good," Greaves replied, a subtle encouragement in his voice. "This won't be a straight line. We'll all need to learn and adjust repeatedly."

He nodded once more and exited quietly, leaving Mehta and Navarro alone to contemplate the long journey ahead.

The battle had only just begun, and they'd already lost the first skirmish.

Transformation Takeaways: Memo to Leadership

To: Thomas Greaves, CEO

From: Elena Navarro, Chief Sustainability Officer, and Vikram Mehta, Chief AI Officer

Date: December 2025

Subject: Reflections on Initial Steps in the Twin Transformation

✓ What Worked

- **Clear strategic framing (Twin Transformation).**
  The articulation of AI and sustainability as mutually reinforcing imperatives, rather than separate trends, provided a compelling narrative that helped win initial board approval.
- **Strong executive leadership and vision.**
  Your direct engagement with the board, and your positioning of sustainability and AI as commercial necessities rather than moral obligations, helped to build key board member support.
- **Physical co-location and structural integration efforts.**
  Bringing AI and sustainability teams together physically and operationally helped to begin the slow work of breaking down cultural and organizational silos.
- **Audit and transparency.**
  The comprehensive internal audit identified real inefficiencies (>$300M in annual waste), giving both credibility to the transformation and urgency to address structural fragmentation.
- **Joint innovation governance.**
  The proposal of an Innovation Task Force and co-owned innovation lab, with embedded KPIs and cross-functional membership, laid the groundwork for scalable collaboration.
- **Strategic positioning of sustainability.**
  The reframing of sustainability as a performance enabler with lower capital costs, reduced compliance risk, improved margins, was crucial in starting to win over internal doubters.

✘ What Didn't Work

- **Boardroom buy-in was partial, not unified.**
  Despite formal approval, some board members appeared unconvinced, especially about sustainability. Their tacit resistance has since bled into the broader executive culture.
- **Fragmentation of internal capabilities.**
  The audit revealed deep organizational silos, duplicated efforts, and lack of cross-team visibility. Nearly all AI and sustainability initiatives had been developed in isolation, reducing potential impact.
- **Cultural resistance from executive leadership team.**
  The first executive meeting revealed entrenched opposition, particularly from Operations (LaPlante), IT (Fernandes), and Finance (Svensson), who see the transformation as a costly distraction or territorial threat.
- **Lack of immediate results to defuse skepticism.**
  Financial pressures and past project failures have created a "show-me" culture. Without early wins, default resistance is calcifying into active obstruction.
- **Misalignment on language and priorities.**
  Early collaboration between the sustainability and AI teams was marred by different mental models, vocabularies, and work cadences, limiting early momentum and reinforcing team-level divisions.
- **Shadow governance concerns.**
  Tensions with the CIO surfaced immediately, with perceived overreach from the AI office. Similar concerns may emerge across other functions unless roles and decision rights are clarified.
- **Absence of a unified change management strategy.**
  No coordinated internal messaging or engagement plan has been deployed to support cultural adoption. The result: confusion, doubt, and territorialism at the leadership level.

- **High external pressure, low internal readiness.**
  With CoolTech now marketing a fully integrated AI + ESG solution, the risk of competitive displacement is real, but internal capabilities are still catching up, and investor confidence remains fragile.

📚 Lessons Learned

- **Twin transformations require a unifying strategic narrative.**
  Positioning AI and sustainability as interdependent drivers of competitiveness, not isolated initiatives, helps overcome the 'either/or' mindset and secures more strategic alignment.
- **Visionary leadership must be matched with political navigation.**
  Bold ideas need not only clarity and conviction but also early, deliberate efforts to bring doubters along, especially board members and function heads who control key resources.
- **Early structural moves send strong cultural signals.**
  Creating high-profile, empowered roles (like CAIO and CSO) legitimizes transformation. But success hinges on clearly defined mandates and coordination with existing power centers (e.g. CIO, COO).
- **Execution starts with unglamorous integration.**
  Break down silos between tech, sustainability, operations, and finance from day one. Without cross-functional governance, even well-funded efforts will underperform or conflict.
- **Skepticism thrives without early wins.**
  In high-pressure environments, quick, measurable results are essential to build internal momentum and credibility. Translate bold visions into pilot projects with fast ROI.
- **Shared language is not optional.**
  Bridging the vocabulary and mindset gaps between technical and sustainability teams is a prerequisite for collaboration. Misunderstandings around priorities and metrics can quickly stall progress.

- **Sustainability gains attention when framed as business risk or reward.**
  Environmental goals should be positioned in terms of business performance, like enhanced revenues, cost control, competitive differentiation, and access to capital, not just ethics or branding.
- **Middle managers are often the frontline of resistance.**
  Even with board approval, entrenched leadership (e.g. operations, finance, IT) will resist unless they see direct value. Engage them early, listen actively, and build incentives into the transformation.
- **Governance without clarity breeds turf war.**
  Ambiguous control over infrastructure, data, and budgets leads to internal conflict. Clearly delineate roles and decision-making authority across new and legacy teams.
- **Open innovation accelerates credibility and momentum.**
  Inviting external partners, startups, and researchers into the transformation process reinforces a culture of learning, expands ideation, and signals seriousness to internal cynics.
- **Transformation is emotional as much as strategic.**
  People's identities are tied to how things have always been done. Recognize and address the fear, pride, and uncertainty that come with disruptive change.

Elena & Vikram

ACT 2

EARLY CHALLENGES

Chapter 6

BUILDING AN
AI SUSTAINABILITY FOUNDATION

Integration begins not with code or carbon,
but with trust.

Fixing a Starting Point

Vikram Mehta and Elena Navarro sat across from each other in a conference room bathed in early morning light, reviewing the latest reports. Their mandate was clear: lay the foundation for AI-driven sustainability at ThermaDynamics. The challenge, however, was where to start.

Navarro flipped through the report, her eyes lingering on the projected resource needs. "This won't come cheap," she said, her tone matter of fact. "New AI systems, retrofitting factories, training programs, it's a massive upfront investment."

Mehta nodded in agreement. "True, but the cost of falling behind is higher. If we get this right, the savings from efficiency and new revenue streams will outweigh the initial hit. We just need to convince the board it's worth the gamble."

He looked at the spreadsheet between them. "But, what's our first move? Scope 3 emissions? That's where most of the environmental impact is: our suppliers, our logistics, our customers' energy use."

Navarro shook her head. "If we start there, we'll fail."

Mehta looked up. "How do you figure?"

She tapped the paper. "You know what kills every big sustainability initiative? Too much ambition. Not enough quick wins. If we go straight for carbon neutrality, we'll run into cost concerns, supply chain resistance, and operational pushback. We must start with what leadership cares about - efficiency, flexibility, and cost reduction. If we win those battles, sustainability follows."

"Moreover, the IoT sensors we installed years ago are collecting data, but it's a mess: fragmented, inconsistent, and spread across silos. We need clean, accessible data before AI can do anything meaningful."

Mehta sighed, tapping his pen. "That's the dirty secret of AI. Garbage in, garbage out. Our first step isn't building models; it's fixing the data infrastructure. That means integrating those IoT feeds, standardizing formats, and getting IT on board."

Mehta leaned back, considering. "So, we frame this as an operations upgrade, not a sustainability initiative?"

"Not just operations," Navarro corrected. "It's also about making our products better and smarter. The future isn't just about making our factories greener, it's about making our systems more intelligent. AI-powered cooling, adaptive energy management, real-time optimization for buildings and industrial sites; if we do this right, our products won't just meet sustainability standards, they'll drive demand because they cut costs and improve performance."

Mehta nodded, the bigger picture was coming into view. "Instead of selling sustainability, we sell intelligence: smarter factories, smarter products, and smarter energy use."

"Exactly," Navarro confirmed. "When we cut energy waste, it lowers costs. When we use AI to optimize production, it improves efficiency. When we design products that help customers reduce their own emissions and energy bills, it makes us indispensable. The fact is that these things also reduce our footprint, but if we sell sustainability first, people will see it as an expense instead of an investment."

Mehta smirked. "We Trojan-horse sustainability inside a business transformation?"

Navarro grinned. "Call it what you want. But my own bitter experience tells me that's how we win."

Mehta exhaled, flipping through a document on supply chain emissions. "I get it. Scope 3 is a black hole. Too many variables, too many external dependencies. If we chase it now, we'll never get anything off the ground."

Navarro nodded. "Exactly. If we try to fix what's outside our control before fixing what's in our hands, we'll drown in complexity. We need quick, measurable wins, things we can prove work, fast."

She tapped the table, bringing the conversation back into focus. "That starts with Scope 1: our own factories, production lines, and equipment. If we optimize those, we don't just improve sustainability KPIs, we cut waste, lower costs, and show the board that AI-driven efficiency delivers real results."

"OK, scope 1 it is," Mehta added, "and let's start with the transparency problem. We can't find solutions until we know where the problems are, and that requires measurement and analysis. This is an area where digital and AI can help."

These were pivotal decisions. Instead of tackling the full spectrum of emissions at once - Scope 1, Scope 2 (indirect emissions from purchased electricity), and Scope 3 (supply chain and product lifecycle emissions), they would start with Scope 1. This would allow them to build internal momentum, gather the right data, and demonstrate success before expanding their focus.

Measuring Scope 1 Emissions

While Mehta's team focused on capturing data and refining AI models for efficiency, Navarro's team tackled the measurement problem. Until now, emissions tracking had been scattered across spreadsheets, outdated software, and manual reporting.

"We need real-time emissions monitoring," Navarro told her sustainability leads. "No more estimations. No more reactive reporting. We track, we analyze, and we act."

Mehta's and Navarro's teams deployed multiple types of sensors across the company's factories and offices. These included quantum sensors, tiny marvels leveraging subatomic precision, tested in a pilot to explore their potential for uncovering inefficiencies missed by traditional sensors. The sensors fed highly accurate data into the systems Mehta's team was developing, enabling AI to detect patterns and suggest reductions.

Early results from these sensors were startling:
- Factory gas furnace emissions were 9% higher than reported, due to inefficiencies in combustion cycles. One of the AI tools Mehta's team had built suggested adjusting burn rates, cutting CO_2 output.
- Compressed air leaks, often overlooked, accounted for 4% of total energy waste.
- Most of the carbon was leaving through exhaust systems. Automated carbon capture integration into these systems could reduce factory emissions by 5%.

"This isn't just compliance," Navarro said in a meeting with Mehta. "This is a business advantage. If we cut emissions while cutting costs, we do more than just meet regulations."

Deliberate Exclusions: No Scope 2 or 3

Despite their progress, one decision remained controversial: They would not focus on Scope 2 or 3 emissions, yet.

Katarina Svensson, the CFO, challenged them in a leadership meeting. "Why aren't we looking at purchased electricity? Or supply chain emissions? Investors want full ESG reporting."

Navarro was ready for the pushback. "Because if we try to fix everything at once, we'll fail at all of it. We need to tackle Scope 1 first, then scale what works."

Mehta backed her up. "AI thrives on data. We control Scope 1 emissions directly, so we can refine our models and prove cost savings. Once we have that credibility, we expand."

Greaves nodded in approval. "Focus is key. Win the battles you can control before expanding the war."

Digital Twins: The Key to Optimization

To execute their vision, they needed a testbed, a way to simulate and measure sustainability efforts before committing to costly rollouts. One answer lay in digital twin technology.

Digital twins are real-time virtual replicas of physical assets. They had already been used by ThermaDynamics in a limited capacity to optimize manufacturing production schedules and predict maintenance failures. Mehta had been working on expanding the digital twin program to map and reduce emissions in real time.

Mehta tapped his screen, pulling up a schematic of ThermaDynamics' Texas manufacturing plant. "We create a full-scale digital twin of this facility, feed it live operational data, and layer in AI to analyze inefficiencies. Then we start testing interventions before implementing them physically."

Navarro saw the potential immediately. "If we run simulations, we'll know exactly which changes will have the biggest impact before we touch a single machine. No disruptions, no wasted investment."

The digital twin project launched with a three-phase approach:
- Baseline modeling: capturing real-time data on energy use, emissions, and equipment performance.
- AI simulation: running virtual scenarios to test emission reduction strategies.
- Live optimization: deploying AI-driven recommendations back into the real-world plant.
- Within weeks, early insights were pouring in. The digital twin identified excessive energy waste during non-peak hours, recommending automated power scaling that could reduce emissions by 12% without affecting production. It also flagged inefficiencies in factory ventilation systems, suggesting adjustments that cut cooling energy use by 18%.

Laying the Foundation for Expansion

By the end of the quarter, ThermaDynamics had a fully functional AI sustainability platform for Scope 1 emissions. The digital twin had already identified inefficiencies that cut 15% of operational carbon output, and projections indicated that the number could reach 25% within a year.

More importantly, the framework was scalable.

Navarro leaned back in her chair after reviewing the latest feedback. "See better. Act better. Scale better. That's the sequence we need to follow. First, we need to increase transparency and follow the data trail. Then we adjust to improve outcomes on a case-by-case basis. Finally, when we know what works, we expand the solutions across the company. The foundation is set. Now we build the future on top of it."

Mehta grinned. "And when we're ready for Scope 2 and 3, we won't just measure emissions. We'll eliminate them."

Navarro glanced at him, then back at the reports. "Before we expand, let's make sure every process in our operations is optimized. We prove this model works internally before scaling it outward."

Mehta nodded. "Of course. If we standardize AI-driven efficiency across our internal systems, we build credibility and eliminate some of the doubts from leadership. That's how we make sure this transformation sticks."

The twin transformation had begun, now with a precise focus - fixing what was within their control before pushing outward.

Chapter 7

THE BOARDROOM BATTLE

*Sometimes progress depends on who speaks last,
and how long the silence lingers.*

A High-Stakes Meeting
The first major test of their vision came during the next Board of Directors meeting. Vikram Mehta and Elena Navarro were invited by Greaves to present their proposal for AI-driven energy optimization across ThermaDynamics' factory network.

As they took their seats in the boardroom, the weight of expectation settled over them. The recent financial downturn loomed large. Revenues were down, margins were tightening, and the stock price had taken a hit. Inside the room, the mood was tense, the board's collective patience running thin.

This was not a room eager to entertain bold, long-term visions.

Still, Mehta and Navarro had come prepared. AI and sustainability, they argued, were not distractions from financial recovery, they were the key to driving efficiency, cost savings, and long-term resilience.

"This isn't just about sustainability," Mehta explained, clicking to the first slide. "It's about smarter operations. Our analysis shows that AI-driven optimization can reduce energy expenses by up to 20% annually. This translates to an estimated $200 million in cost savings company-wide, based on scaling our Texas digital twin pilot results across our global facilities."

He paused, letting the numbers settle in.

Richard Steele leaned back in his chair, folding his arms as he considered Mehta and Navarro's proposal. His expression was unreadable, but when he finally spoke, his voice carried the weight of decades in the industry.

"You know what I keep coming back to?" he said, looking around the boardroom. "This company exists because people need to control temperature. The hotter the world gets, the more essential we become. That's not an opinion, it's reality. Air conditioning turned the American South into an economic powerhouse. It made entire industries like pharmaceuticals, aerospace, and computing possible. The world relies on what we do."

He gestured toward the slide deck still glowing on the screen. "And now you're telling me that our future depends on making those systems so efficient that they run less? That the best thing we can do for the planet is to reduce the very demand that keeps us in business? Help me understand that math."

Silence stretched across the room. Even Greaves didn't immediately respond.

Mehta shifted in his seat, preparing to counter, but Steele wasn't done. He tapped his knuckles against the table, eyes hardening.

"You also want me to believe that some algorithm is going to magically solve this contradiction for us? That AI will make us greener, cheaper, and more profitable all at the same time? This sounds like tech fantasy," he scoffed. "Factories aren't software. You can't just optimize them like a spreadsheet. We've been running a finely tuned operation for decades, and it works. What you're proposing is a disruption we can't afford."

Steele's voice carried an air of finality, as if the matter had been settled. But his resistance ran deeper than skepticism. To him, talk of AI-powered efficiency was little more than a costly distraction when what they really needed was a turnaround.

James Morrison nodded in agreement, his expression one of thinly veiled exasperation. "Changing factory operations isn't like updating a phone app," he said, his voice edged with impatience. "We operate on strict production schedules. If AI tells us to change energy use patterns mid-shift and it slows down the line by even 2%, we lose millions. You're talking about theoretical benefits at the risk of $300 million in annual production value."

Mehta glanced at Navarro, who had been watching the board members carefully. The resistance was coming from different angles, some from fear of disruption, others from financial caution, and a few from outright disbelief.

Deepening the Debate

As tensions in the room grew, Mehta and Navarro fought to maintain their composure. They had anticipated resistance, but the intensity of the pushback was stronger than expected. They knew that unless they could demonstrate the feasibility of their proposal in a way that resonated with the board's financial priorities, their initiative would be dead on arrival.

"We understand your concerns," Navarro interjected, her voice steady despite the mounting pressure. "That's why we've built this model on data-backed projections. The industrial sector is evolving, and AI-driven optimization is no longer experimental, it's an operational necessity. Companies that fail to embrace it will see their margins erode as energy costs continue to rise."

She pulled up a slide showcasing case studies from competitors who had implemented similar strategies and achieved up to 20% reductions in energy expenditures within a three-year window. She further highlighted that AI-driven energy management had helped some firms maintain regulatory compliance, avoiding fines that could cost millions annually.

Despite her compelling argument, Steele remained unconvinced.

"Regulations change, but our fundamentals have always been the same," he said, shaking his head. "We don't chase trends, we build on proven principles."

Seeing an opportunity, Mehta shifted his approach.

"This isn't about chasing trends," he countered. "It's about staying ahead of disruption. Look at the increasing volatility in global energy markets. Our operational energy expenditure currently exceeds $150 million per year. If we do nothing, our costs could rise by another 20% in the next five years due to inflation and increased regulatory pressure. We need proactive solutions."

A clipped sigh betrayed Steele's frustration, but he said nothing further.

A Shifting Focus

Greaves, who had largely remained silent, intervened at last.

"We need to be mindful of the current business climate," he said, his tone even. "Our investors are looking for short-term performance, not long-term bets. If we had strong revenue growth, we could afford to take more risks. But the reality is, we're under pressure to deliver results now."

His words landed like a hammer.

Mehta stiffened in his seat. This wasn't just about the board's uncertainty, this was about shifting priorities. The very leadership that had championed their efforts was now recalibrating.

The rules had changed.

Steele seized the moment.

"I think that settles it," he said, leaning back in his chair. "We don't need another experimental initiative right now. We need to focus on fixing the basics: sales, quality, and market confidence."

The words stung. Mehta stole a glance at Navarro, who remained expressionless, her fingers resting lightly on the edge of the table. He knew that behind her calm exterior, her mind was already calculating the next move.

Reframing the Strategy

Navarro took a deep breath before speaking. "We understand the concerns," she said, choosing her words carefully. "That's why we're not proposing an immediate overhaul, we're suggesting a pilot project. Low risk, high visibility, and immediate cost savings."

She pulled up a slide detailing a three-month pilot program at a single facility.

- Focus: AI-powered energy efficiency.
- Target savings: $2 million in reduced energy costs per year.
- Projected efficiency gains: 12% reduction in peak-hour consumption.
- No disruptions: AI would run in the background, optimizing without interfering with production schedules.

Mehta turned to Steele.

"This isn't about adding complexity," Mehta said. "This is about survival. If we do nothing, our costs could easily increase by 20% over the next five years."

The boardroom fell silent.

Finally, Steele sighed. "Fine. You get your pilot. But one thing is clear - this is not the company's focus right now. If this distracts from quarterly performance, it's done."

A Tentative First Step

While it was not the full endorsement Mehta and Navarro had hoped for, it was a crucial first step. The pilot would focus on:

- AI-optimized energy management: testing predictive algorithms for real-time energy adjustments at a single factory, with a goal of cutting energy costs by $2 million a year.
- Sustainable supply chain analytics: Implementing machine learning models to track suppliers' sustainability compliance and identify cost-effective eco-friendly alternatives, reducing procurement inefficiencies by 14%.
- Workforce training and adaptation: Introducing AI-assisted tools to factory floor employees and tracking engagement and productivity impact, ensuring alignment with operational workflows.

The approval was hard-won, but Mehta and Navarro knew their real challenge lay ahead. The pilot needed to succeed, not just in theory, but in measurable results that would silence their critics. As they left the boardroom, Mehta turned to Navarro and said, "Failure is not an option."

Chapter 8

THE AI-POWERED PILOT BEGINS

*The future doesn't arrive with certainty,
it begins as an experiment.*

From Simulation to Reality

The board had approved the twin transformation pilot, but it was clear that doubts remained. Vikram Mehta and Elena Navarro had managed to secure a cautious green light, but it wasn't an outright endorsement. The message from the leadership team was clear: If the pilot caused disruptions or failed to show measurable returns, the project would be dead before it had a chance to scale.

This was why Mehta insisted on de-risking the rollout with a digital twin of the Texas manufacturing facility, simulating AI-driven optimizations before implementing them in the real world. Every machine had a digital counterpart, all running on real-time data collected from sensors across the factory floor.

Fortunately, much of the groundwork was already in place. Years earlier, ThermaDynamics had begun installing IoT sensors as part of an earlier automation push, though the data had never been fully utilized. Now, Mehta saw an opportunity to repurpose this dormant infrastructure. With his previous experience in building digital twins, he knew exactly how to accelerate deployment - leveraging existing data streams, refining AI models from past projects, and integrating new analytics layers without having to start from scratch. What would normally take six months could now be done in a fraction of the time.

At the first simulation review meeting, Mehta stood in front of a massive screen, watching the AI dashboard hum with real-time data from the Texas plant factory floor. The IoT sensors, now seamlessly integrated after weeks of infrastructure upgrades, delivered clean, consistent data streams, unified across the company's systems. "This is what we needed," he told his lead data scientist, a grin spreading across his face. "With this data foundation, our predictive models can finally work at full precision. We're not guessing anymore, we're optimizing."

The AI had already begun detecting inefficiencies such as machines running unnecessarily during shift transitions, excessive HVAC energy use, and maintenance bottlenecks.

"This is where we waste the most energy... With AI-driven scheduling, we can reduce this waste by up to a fifth without affecting output, as proven in our Texas simulations."

Fred LaPlante, the ever-skeptical COO, frowned. "A simulation is nice, but we run a real factory, not a video game. I don't want to make operational changes based on theory."

Navarro stepped in. "Fred, this isn't theory, it's a controlled prediction model. We're using this so we don't experiment on the factory floor. If something doesn't work, we find out here first."

To prove the point, Mehta ran a stress-test simulation, mimicking an unexpected equipment failure at peak production. The results were striking:

- Without AI, the downtime would cost $100,000 per hour in lost productivity.
- With AI-driven predictive maintenance, the system flagged the issue six hours before failure, triggering a scheduled repair and avoiding the loss entirely.

At this, LaPlante leaned forward slightly, and for once, looked more intrigued than dismissive.

The digital twin demonstrated three key insights:

- Energy efficiency improvements of up to 20% by optimizing machine scheduling and HVAC loads, consistent with the early pilot findings.
- A 28% reduction in unexpected equipment failures through AI-driven predictive maintenance, with downtime costing $100,000 per hour in lost productivity, reflecting the real-world impact.
- Seamless integration of AI into workflows, proving that the factory wouldn't experience disruptive downtime.

With these results in hand, Mehta and Navarro knew they weren't walking in blind. But as they finalized preparations for the live deployment, one thing was clear, simulations could only take them so far. The true test was about to begin.

The AI Needs an Edge

Even with a successful digital twin simulation, Mehta and Navarro faced a critical hurdle: Speed. Their twin transformation system needed to make split-second decisions to keep the Texas factory running smoothly, but relying on cloud computing introduced frustrating delays. In manufacturing, even a one-second lag could mean the difference between catching a looming equipment failure early or watching an entire production line grind to a halt, costing the company thousands.

Mehta paced the pre-launch technical briefing room as he considered the problem. "We can't afford to wait for data to ping back and forth to some distant server," he said, his voice tinged with urgency. "If a machine overheats or a power surge hits, we need the AI to act instantly, not after a delay that could shut us down."

Navarro nodded, leaning against the conference table. She understood the stakes, not just for the pilot, but for proving their vision to doubters like Fred LaPlante. "So, how do we fix this?" she asked, her tone practical but probing.

Mehta smiled in response. "We bring the brains closer to the action, right here on the factory floor. It's called edge computing. Instead of sending every piece of data across the internet to a far-off cloud server, we use smart devices right in the factory to process information on the spot. Think of it like having a local coach calling plays during a game, instead of waiting for instructions from headquarters miles away."

Navarro frowned, thinking through the implications. "And what about energy use? AI models eat up an enormous amount of power. How much extra energy will be consumed by processing locally?"

Mehta tapped a few keys, pulling up another data set. "Actually, the opposite. We'll use less. Every time we send data to the cloud, it has to travel through multiple network nodes, burning energy at each step. Running AI models on distant servers means higher computational load, which means more power demand at massive data centers. But by keeping processing on-site with edge devices, we eliminate a huge chunk of that energy use. Less data transmission, fewer redundant computations, and no overreliance on power-hungry remote servers."

Navarro nodded, seeing the broader implications. "In other words, edge computing doesn't just make AI faster, it makes it greener, too?"

"In this case, yes," Mehta said. "It's not just a performance upgrade. It's a sustainability win."

Navarro raised an eyebrow, intrigued. "So, it's like giving the factory its own instant decision-making power."

"Exactly," Mehta replied, pulling up a simple diagram on the screen. A factory floor with small, glowing nodes representing edge devices scattered among machines. "These edge devices handle the heavy lifting locally, crunching data from our IoT sensors in real time. If a conveyor belt starts overheating or a cooling system spikes in power usage, the AI can adjust ventilation or power settings immediately. This means no waiting, no network bottlenecks."

To demonstrate, Mehta ran a quick side-by-side comparison on the digital twin simulation. He showed what happens when they rely on cloud processing: the AI detected an overheating issue in a core assembly unit, but the system had to send data to a remote server, wait for analysis, and then receive instructions. In the simulation, this took more than five seconds. On the factory floor, that delay could mean a costly shutdown or missed opportunity to prevent damage.

Then he switched to the edge-powered model. The same overheating alert popped up, but this time, the AI processed it instantly, adjusting the ventilation system in milliseconds. No lag, no risk of disconnection, just seamless, real-time action.

"This isn't just about speed," Mehta explained, his voice rising with conviction. "It's about reliability. If the internet goes down, which is a real risk in a factory environment, the edge system keeps running. No unexpected shutdowns, no loss of optimization."

Navarro saw the bigger picture immediately. "And from a sustainability angle, this cuts down on the energy we'd waste sending data back and forth to the cloud. Less data transmission means lower emissions and lower costs, a win for both our goals."

Fred LaPlante, who had been listening distrustfully from the back of the room, leaned forward, his arms uncrossing for the first time. "So, you're telling me we're not handing control over to some offsite data center we can't monitor?" he asked, his voice gruff but curious. "I admit I am intrigued, as long as it doesn't slow down my production lines."

Mehta met his gaze, sensing an opening. "It won't, Fred. Edge computing keeps decision-making local and lightning-fast. We're not disrupting your operations, we're making them more resilient."

"Edge computing gives us real-time insights where we need them most," Mehta continued. "But it's not either-or. It's about putting the right workload in the right place."

No single computing model could solve all of ThermaDynamics' challenges. Edge systems brought responsiveness but lacked the muscle to run advanced simulations. Cloud infrastructure provided that power, but it also introduced latency. The real transformation came from blending both.

"We need a hybrid approach," Mehta said. "Edge computing keeps things moving in real time which is crucial for minimizing downtime on the factory floor. But for the heavy lifting - predictive maintenance across multiple lines, supply chain optimization, emissions forecasting - we need the centralized cloud. It's got the computing muscle and can integrate data from every sensor to give us the full picture."

Navarro raised an eyebrow. "Sounds like we're splitting the workload. Will that complicate things?"

"It's a balancing act," Mehta admitted. "Edge and centralized systems must talk to each other seamlessly, or we risk latency and data mismatches. But if we get it right, we combine the speed of edge with the smarts of the cloud. That's how we make this pilot a game-changer."

With that, the team had found their edge, both literally and figuratively. The decision to integrate AI-powered edge devices into the pilot facility gave ThermaDynamics a competitive advantage no other firm had yet deployed at scale. It wasn't just about technology; it was about proving to LaPlante, Steele, and the rest that their vision could work without sacrificing the reliability ThermaDynamics had built its reputation on.

Now, with the digital twin tested and edge computing in place, ThermaDynamics was ready. The pilot would be more than an experiment, it would be a revolution in real-time, AI-driven sustainability. But Mehta and Navarro knew even the most brilliant technology couldn't shield them from the human challenges still ahead.

Chapter 9

THE PILOT'S GROWING PAINS

When innovation meets inertia,
only persistence survives.

Early Hurdles in Factory Optimization

The factory floor at ThermaDynamics' pilot site was buzzing, not with excitement, but with doubt and frustration. The company's first AI-driven energy optimization initiative was supposed to prove that digital transformation could enhance efficiency while reducing costs. Instead, it had been met with immediate resistance.

Workers, already wary of automation, viewed the new IoT-enabled monitoring systems as an existential threat. Rumors spread rapidly. "They're just going to use this data to replace us with machines," murmured one technician. The local union representative confronted management, demanding reassurances about job security. HR, led by Saskia Schmidt, immediately sought to mitigate fears by organizing town hall meetings to explain that the technology was intended to assist, not replace, workers.

"I've been running this line for fifteen years," grumbled Hector Ramirez, a senior machine operator. "Now some software is going to tell me how to do my job?"

Vikram Mehta stood beside the factory control panel, watching Ramirez hesitate over an AI suggestion to adjust a machine's power settings. "You're not just following the system," Mehta said, pointing to the override option. "We've built it so your experience guides the AI, it's human-in-the-loop, putting you in control."

Ramirez nodded, testing the change manually, and a flicker of trust crossed his face as production stabilized.

Others worried about surveillance. The IoT sensors tracked energy use in real-time, but to workers, it felt like they were being monitored every second.

"This system is supposed to 'help' us, but all I see is it tracking every move we make," said Shelley Carter, a technician on the assembly line. "Next thing we know, they'll be cutting our shifts because the algorithm says we're not 'efficient' enough."

Faced with a mounting backlash, HR Head Saskia Schmidt stepped in. She urged Mehta and Navarro to shift their approach before the factory floor turned entirely against them.

To ease tensions, Mehta and Navarro organized hands-on training sessions, where engineers demonstrated how AI tools optimized energy use without interfering with workers' expertise. The company also introduced a feedback loop, allowing employees to voice concerns and suggest adjustments.

Despite HR's efforts, worker morale continued to drop as stories of previous automation-led layoffs in the industry circulated among employees. Productivity slowed as some workers deliberately resisted the technology, reverting to manual processes or finding excuses to avoid interaction with the AI-powered systems. Factory supervisors reported that downtime incidents had risen by 15% in just three weeks, exacerbating existing inefficiencies instead of solving them.

The concern extended beyond the shop floor. Mid-level managers, responsible for hitting production targets, voiced concerns that they had no control over the AI-driven system. "We're being asked to trust a black box," one factory supervisor complained. "If something goes wrong, it's our necks on the line, not the algorithm's." This sentiment led to a dangerous feedback loop: operators avoided interacting with the AI, which prevented it from gathering the necessary data to improve, which in turn led to continued inefficiencies.

The technology itself was not making things any easier. The AI systems, still in their early learning phases, were generating erratic power consumption recommendations. Several times, production lines were shut down due to miscalculations, leading to costly delays. An unexpected system override during peak hours caused a two-hour full-line stoppage, resulting in an estimated loss of $80,000. Each malfunction fueled LaPlante's frustration.

"This is exactly why we don't gamble with our core business," LaPlante scoffed in a leadership meeting, eyes blazing. "Every hour a production line goes down costs us massively. How many more 'learning experiences' can we afford?"

Navarro's Breaking Point

The factory floor was quiet, save for the hum of machines running at half capacity. Elena Navarro stood at the edge of the AI control panel, arms crossed, jaw tight. Another setback. Another inefficiency flagged by the system but left unaddressed due to resistance from the operations team.

She had seen the pattern repeat itself, workers ignoring AI recommendations, mid-level managers pushing back on automated adjustments, senior leadership demanding results while refusing to change workflows. It was a mess.

"This isn't working," she muttered under her breath.

Vikram Mehta barely looked up from his tablet. "We adjust. We optimize. That's the process."

Navarro turned to face him, her frustration boiling over. "You think this is just another process? Another algorithm that needs tweaking?" Her voice was sharp, cutting through the stale air of the operations hub. "This isn't just about numbers, Vikram. These are people's jobs. This is their future."

Mehta sighed, rubbing his temples. "I get it, but you're acting like we can control every variable overnight."

"No, you don't get it." Navarro's voice wavered, but she steadied herself. "My father ran a manufacturing plant. He built it from the ground up, kept it running for 30 years. And then, when new environmental regulations came in, he couldn't keep up. He had to shut it down. He lost everything." She exhaled sharply, as if pushing out a weight she had carried for years.

Mehta remained silent, watching her intently.

"I was just a teenager," she continued, her tone quieter now. "I saw him go from being respected in the industry to drowning in paperwork and compliance rules that were meant to help the planet but ended up crippling his business. He had to lay off workers, people who had been with him since the start. Our family lost everything. And no one cared because 'sustainability' was supposed to be the future." She stretched out her fingers. "Of course I'm not against sustainability. But I promised myself I'd prove that it doesn't have to mean shutting people out of their own industries. That's why I took this job." She shook her head. "And right now, it feels like we're failing."

Mehta's Confession

For once, Mehta didn't have a counterpoint. He stared at the factory floor, watching the workers moving between stations, hesitant around the AI-driven systems.

"I know what failure looks like too," he said finally. "My first startup was built on AI. We had funding, talent, the best models money could buy. We thought we were revolutionizing the market. But we weren't solving a real problem. We were just... innovating for the sake of it."

Navarro frowned, but she didn't interrupt.

"We burned through millions in funding before we realized we were chasing a tech dream that had no foundation in reality. Investors pulled out. The company collapsed. And I was left wondering what the hell I'd been doing." He exhaled, staring at the screen in front of him. "I told myself if I ever got another shot, I'd build something that actually mattered. Something that wasn't just flashy AI for the sake of it but something that made a real impact."

He glanced at her. "That's why I'm here."

A long silence stretched between them.

Finally, Navarro shook her head, a hint of a smile forming. "So, you're telling me you're not just here to automate me out of a job?"

Mehta snorted. "Not unless you keep making my job harder."

For the first time in what seemed like days, they both laughed, just a little.

CFO Scrutiny and Financial Justifications

If the technical failures weren't enough, Katarina Svensson, the CFO, was growing increasingly impatient. She had supported the project under the condition that it would yield quantifiable cost savings within the first six months. So far, those savings had not materialized.

"I need hard numbers," Svensson said in a tense video call from the Maidenhead office. "We projected a 10% reduction in energy costs, which should translate to at least $2.5 million in annual savings. Where are we on that? Because right now, I only see mounting costs."

Mehta explained that AI models required continuous data refinement to optimize performance, and that energy savings would ramp up once the system adapted to factory patterns. But Svensson was unmoved. "We can't tell investors that we're spending millions on something that 'should' work in the future. I need a breakdown of expected savings month by month, not vague assurances."

Navarro attempted to bolster their case by highlighting long-term sustainability benefits. "Our predictive models estimate that, once stabilized, we can reduce CO_2 emissions by 30,000 metric tons per year, improving our regulatory standing and positioning us for green incentives."

Svensson shook her head. "That's great for PR and compliance, but we're in the red on this project right now."

Damage Control and Adjustments

Realizing that they were losing support, Mehta and Navarro worked around the clock with their teams to stabilize the system.

The first breakthrough came through algorithm refinements. By partnering with Fernandes' IT department, they fine-tuned the AI prediction systems to reduce false shutdowns by 70% within two weeks. The technical teams reconfigured data models to incorporate real-time human override options, allowing experienced operators to prevent unnecessary disruptions. This hybrid approach preserved the benefits of AI while acknowledging the value of human expertise.

Schmidt's HR team simultaneously launched a comprehensive worker engagement program. The hands-on training initiative demonstrated how IoT tools could improve workflow efficiency rather than replace jobs. Employees were invited to beta-test the system and provide feedback that directly influenced AI-driven recommendations. The program was ambitious, targeting a 40% increase in AI adoption rates over the following quarter.

Rather than focusing exclusively on long-term benefits, Mehta and Navarro identified immediate ROI opportunities. They implemented rapid changes such as recalibrating energy use during non-peak hours, resulting in an 8% immediate reduction in energy waste. Small adjustments to machinery idle time management alone saved $110,000 within the first month - a concrete figure that resonated with the finance department.

The implementation strategy itself underwent revision. Instead of attempting a factory-wide rollout of AI controls at once, they transitioned to a phased implementation approach. Automation was introduced only in low-risk areas first, such as lighting and HVAC energy management. This methodical approach minimized operational disruptions and allowed workers to gradually acclimate to new processes without feeling overwhelmed.

On the financial front, Mehta and Navarro collaborated with Svensson's finance team to create a detailed rolling financial impact report. This document demonstrated how incremental cost savings would scale over time and established quarterly savings goals. The team committed to achieving at least $1 million in reductions by the end of the second quarter, a measurable target that gave the Board concrete metrics to evaluate.

The combined effect of these adjustments began to shift perceptions throughout the organization. Resistance, while still present, had begun to diminish as tangible results emerged. The Texas facility transformation, initially viewed as a liability by many in senior management, was gradually transitioning into a potential model for company-wide implementation.

Chapter 10

A BREAKTHROUGH IN THE MARKET

Proof doesn't end the debate,
but it shifts who controls the narrative.

Voice of the Customer

At a break in the next management team meeting, Serge Closer, Head of Sales, pulled Navarro and Mehta aside. "Could you guys use AI or whatever to make our products more efficient? I love what you're doing with the factory in Texas, but that's operations. If we could cut building heating and cooling energy costs for our customers by 15-20%, that's something I could really sell."

Navarro and Mehta exchanged glances. So far, the twin transformation had been entirely focused on proving the internal business case for AI-driven energy efficiency. Their efforts had centered around optimizing ThermaDynamics' factories, but the pushback from operations, finance, and particularly Fernandes' IT team had slowed progress.

Now, Closer was offering a potential way forward: a market-driven approach.

"Customers are asking for smarter, more sustainable solutions," Closer continued, "and we've been giving them the same old hardware. This might be what we need to set us apart."

It didn't take long for Navarro and Mehta to pivot their strategy. In addition to focusing on internal processes, they also began work on AI-enabled energy efficiency as a value-added feature for customers. If Closer's sales team could show demand, it would be much harder for resisters like LaPlante or Svensson to argue against further investment.

Engineering Breakthrough

Their first step was approaching the Head of R&D, Dr. Helena Yoshida, with data from the Texas facility demonstrating how AI-driven systems had optimized energy consumption. Interested, but unconvinced, Yoshida agreed to a limited collaboration focusing on the company's commercial HVAC units - a product line that had recently experienced quality issues and was in the process of being refreshed.

Due to the increasing pressure from the board, Mehta and Navarro sought rapid, impactful improvements that would demonstrate immediate value. Traditional methods alone weren't delivering the quick results they needed.

One afternoon, while reviewing the latest factory automation challenges, Mehta had an unexpected idea. "What if our solutions are already out there, just in other industries?" he asked, turning towards Navarro and Yoshida. "Perhaps our quickest win could come from outside our walls entirely."

Intrigued, Navarro nodded. "You mean cross-industry innovation?"

"Exactly," Mehta confirmed. "Let's not reinvent the wheel if we don't have to."

Within days, they convened a special cross-industry workshop at ThermaDynamics' innovation lab, inviting Yoshida to co-host the event. Together, they welcomed engineers and operational leads from automotive, aerospace, agriculture, and healthcare sectors to share proven solutions from their fields.

The workshop revealed surprising overlaps. An engineer from an automotive firm described predictive maintenance algorithms originally developed for electric vehicle battery packs. Mehta's eyes widened as he realized these algorithms could significantly improve ThermaDynamics' HVAC system reliability. Meanwhile, Navarro found inspiration from an agricultural firm's IoT-enabled irrigation systems, designed to optimize water use through sensor-driven AI. Yoshida, initially hesitant, grew visibly intrigued by these cross-sector possibilities.

"We could adapt that irrigation logic for HVAC cooling cycles," Navarro said excitedly. "It would optimize energy use by precisely managing cooling in real-time." Yoshida nodded thoughtfully, already visualizing the technical implications.

Within weeks, ThermaDynamics implemented both concepts in a pilot project at the Texas facility. Results were impressive: predictive maintenance algorithms slashed equipment downtime, while the adapted agriculture-inspired cooling optimization reduced energy usage by one sixth.

The ThermaDynamics team identified three key areas for improvement: compressor performance, heat exchange efficiency, and smart load balancing. Mehta's AI specialists developed algorithms that could predict optimal operating parameters based on external conditions, while Yoshida's engineers supported by Navarro's sustainability experts redesigned components to reduce energy consumption and minimize refrigerant requirements.

By then, Navarro and Mehta's partnership had evolved into a twin engine of transformation. Their teams, once reluctant partners mired in friction, now operated as a unified force, seamlessly blending AI innovation with sustainability strategy. What had started as a strained collaboration had hardened into trust, each side anticipating the other's moves, sharpening one another's ideas, and accelerating ThermaDynamics' reinvention. Within five weeks, the team produced a prototype that demonstrated a 23% improvement in energy efficiency compared to the company's current models and a 15% advantage over leading competitors. The AI-enhanced control system continuously adjusted performance parameters based on environmental conditions, occupancy patterns, and time-of-day pricing for electricity.

Picking up from their experiences in the Texas factory, the prototype also addressed a significant market pain point by incorporating predictive maintenance capabilities. Sensors monitored component wear patterns and performance degradation, allowing the system to schedule maintenance before failures occurred. Early calculations suggested this feature alone could reduce customer maintenance costs by up to a third while extending equipment lifespan by 2-3 years.

Equally important was the environmental impact. The redesigned system reduced refrigerant requirements and incorporated components manufactured using recycled materials wherever possible. Navarro's team conducted a full lifecycle analysis that demonstrated a 26% reduction in embedded carbon compared to previous models.

For Yoshida, who had been under pressure to address the quality issues with the commercial line, the collaboration produced tangible benefits. Her team incorporated the improvements into their development roadmap, accelerating plans for the next product generation. She also committed engineering resources to extend similar enhancements across ThermaDynamics' residential portfolio.

With R&D now actively engaged, the foundation was laid for the next critical step: bringing their enhanced products to market. This would require carefully crafted messaging and sales strategies to overcome customer hesitation and capture the potential value they had created.

The Shift to Customer-Focused Innovation

With a portfolio of energy-efficient products close to hand, Mehta and Navarro worked with Closer's team to refine the messaging around ThermaDynamics' AI-driven energy platform. They collaborated with the marketing team to position the solution as a cutting-edge product offering that could differentiate the company in the market.

Marketing produced new case studies, showing hypothetical savings for clients in various industries. They developed customer personas, focusing on real estate developers, commercial landlords, and facilities managers who were under pressure to cut costs while maintaining high operational efficiency.

They also worked on pricing models that would allow businesses to implement the AI-driven systems with minimal upfront costs. Using a performance-based pricing strategy, customers would pay based on the energy savings they actually realized, making the product a low-risk investment.

The sales team ran initial outreach campaigns to test the waters. They leveraged industry events and conferences to gauge interest, quickly identifying high-value leads. Within a few weeks, more than two dozen potential clients had expressed interest, with five requesting detailed proposals.

One of these was Riverview Properties, a major commercial real estate firm considering an upgrade to its building management systems. The stakes were high, securing Riverview as a customer could open doors to other real estate giants.

The First Major Deal – A High-Stakes Pitch

Serge Closer wasted no time setting up a high-profile sales meeting with Riverview Properties, a major commercial real estate firm considering an upgrade to its building management systems. Mehta and Navarro, still battling the scars of their internal struggles, now found themselves on the frontlines of a customer pitch.

Sarah Young, Facilities Manager, and James Patel, CFO, led the Riverview Properties delegation. From the start, misgivings were evident.

"This is a substantial capital investment," Patel pointed out, scanning the pricing proposal. "Why should we take a risk on new AI-driven technology when our current systems are 'good enough'?"

Navarro took a deep breath. They had learned from their internal battles that cost savings were the most convincing argument. "James, the data you shared with us shows that your company spends $12 million annually on energy costs across your commercial properties. Our AI-driven optimization could cut that by at least $2 million a year, and that's just from energy savings. Over the next five years, that's a minimum of $10 million in direct savings."

Mehta backed her up, pulling up predictive analytics. "And that doesn't include maintenance cost reductions. Our AI system uses predictive modeling to prevent equipment failures, reducing maintenance costs by 20-25%. Your operational expenses will decrease, and your building efficiency will go up."

Navarro tapped the screen of her iPad, showing Young and Patel a dashboard where AI suggested energy adjustments for their flagship building. "You're in control," she said. "Our human-in-the-loop design lets you tweak or override AI recommendations based on your expertise, ensuring efficiency without losing your say."

However, Young still looked uncertain. "How can we be sure it works in real-world conditions?"

Closer, sensing the hesitation, jumped in. "We're willing to set up a pilot at one of your flagship buildings for six months, completely risk-free. If you don't see a measurable reduction in energy costs by at least 10%, we'll walk away, no commitment.

The Turning Point

After several more rounds of negotiation, Patel and Young agreed to the pilot. The deal was the first major sale for ThermaDynamics' AI-driven energy platform, valued at $10 million over five years if fully implemented across all Riverview properties.

Internally, the victory shifted perceptions. The AI initiative, once seen as a cost-heavy experiment, was now a market differentiator. With Closer's sales team on board, internal resistance from Svensson and LaPlante weakened. The focus was now on scaling the success story and replicating it across multiple clients.

Turning Customers into Co-Creators of Sustainability

As the company pushed forward, Elena Navarro and Vikram Mehta knew they couldn't achieve lasting sustainability unless their customers were fully onboard. Conventional wisdom had always been that customers passively consumed products designed by companies. But ThermaDynamics was now ready to flip that model on its head.

Mehta had introduced a novel digital initiative he called the 'Open Twin Platform' which was an interactive digital twin accessible directly by existing and potential customers. Through this platform, customers could virtually simulate their buildings or production environments and experiment with different ThermaDynamics products and configurations in real-time.

Early adopters were quickly intrigued. Factory managers could test virtual retrofits to gauge potential energy savings before committing capital. Building administrators began experimenting with AI-driven thermostatic controls, tweaking energy use patterns to see real-time cost impacts.

One morning, Navarro joined Mehta in the innovation lab to review initial customer feedback. "Look at these responses," she said, scrolling through her tablet. "Customers aren't just using this to save costs, they're giving us ideas we never imagined."

Mehta nodded enthusiastically. "It's true co-creation. Customers are tweaking the AI parameters and identifying energy-saving methods we'd overlooked. We already have a dozen actionable insights to feed back into R&D."

But the open innovation model wasn't universally accepted. Fred LaPlante had pushed back, questioning why they were giving customers this much control. "You're asking customers to redesign our products for us?" he complained during a management meeting.

Mehta calmly responded, "We're inviting them to improve their own outcomes, Fred. And each improvement they make enhances their commitment to our solutions."

Elena Navarro continued, her voice measured but steadfast. "Customers are no longer passive consumers; they're active participants in shaping our future. If we harness that effectively, we won't just sell smarter products, we'll build a smarter business."

Scaling the Model for Growth

Mehta and Navarro worked with Closer's team to build a broader strategy for expansion. They identified three additional target industries: industrial manufacturers, data centers, and healthcare facilities, each of which had high energy consumption and strict cost-efficiency mandates.

They also partnered with the legal and finance teams to develop streamlined contract terms that made it easier for customers to sign on without heavy capital expenditures. Subscription-based pricing models were introduced, making the AI-driven platform a service rather than a one-time purchase, ensuring recurring revenue.

Meanwhile, Mehta's team accelerated R&D efforts to fine-tune the AI's ability to adapt to different building types, aiming to reduce setup times from six months to three, making the solution more attractive to clients with tight turnaround times.

As the team prepared for the next round of customer engagements, they knew they had only scratched the surface. Riverview's results would be closely monitored, and their ability to replicate success would determine whether this was a short-term win or the beginning of a major transformation for ThermaDynamics.

The internal skeptics were still watching, waiting for any sign of failure. But for the first time, Mehta and Navarro weren't just defending the twin transformation, they were proving that it could be the company's future.

Rethinking the Business Model

Inside the ThermaDynamics conference room, a strategy meeting with Serge Closer and Thomas Greaves had taken an interesting turn. A rough diagram was sketched on a whiteboard, outlining a radical shift in strategy.

Mehta leaned forward, marker in hand, and posed a question that made Serge raise an eyebrow.

"What if we didn't sell air conditioners at all?" The idea hung in the air for a moment.

Greaves tilted his head, intrigued but cautious. "What do you mean?" he asked.

Mehta pointed to the whiteboard.

"Right now, our most advanced units, the ones with AI-driven efficiency and lower energy consumption, are also our most expensive. That means the businesses and communities that would benefit the most from them often can't afford them. So, what if we installed them for free?"

Closer leaned back, confused by this turn of events.

"And how does that generate revenue?"

Mehta didn't hesitate.

"By shifting from a product sale to a service model. Instead of customers paying for the hardware, they pay for the outcome, a guaranteed indoor temperature of, say, 22 degrees Celsius. We take full responsibility for maintaining that temperature while using AI to optimize efficiency. Every aspect, cooling cycles, predictive maintenance, demand-response energy pricing, is managed intelligently to minimize costs. The less energy the system consumes, the more profitable the model becomes."

Thomas Greaves, who had been listening intently from his seat, adjusted his posture, his expression neutral.

"So instead of selling a product, we sell comfort?"

Mehta nodded.

"Exactly. Customers don't worry about energy consumption, only that their space stays at the agreed temperature. And because the system is AI-driven, we have every opportunity to make cooling as efficient as possible."

Closer shook his head, still unconvinced. "That's a complete departure from the current business model. We're a manufacturer, Vikram."

Mehta turned toward him.

"We still will be. Look, traditionally, an air conditioning unit is a one-time sale. This model turns it into a recurring revenue stream, a subscription-based service with predictable cash flow."

Greaves cleared his throat.

"And what about the initial costs? We'd be installing expensive units without immediate payback."

Navarro stepped in.

"Not necessarily a risk if approached strategically. Think about solar companies that lease panels and charge for the energy generated. Or cloud computing; customers don't buy servers, they pay for computing power. If we control the equipment, we control long-term profitability."

Closer exhaled, rubbing his chin.

"That still leaves customer acquisition. How do we convince them?"

Navarro gestured toward the board.

"That's the beauty of it. This could extend beyond corporate buildings. Heat waves are getting worse, and this is hitting hard, particularly in low-income communities. Reliable cooling is becoming a necessity. If the cost barrier is removed and replaced with a low monthly fee, deployment becomes scalable. There are even potential partnerships with governments and NGOs to support it."

Silence stretched for a moment.

Greaves finally spoke. "This could be... big."

Mehta grinned. "It's the future."

Greaves glanced around the room, then nodded. "Alright, model it out and get back to me. For now, it stays between us, OK?"

Navarro, Mehta, and Closer spent the next several days refining the idea, turning it into a concrete business case. They poured over financial models, market analyses, and risk assessments, ensuring every angle was covered. The result was a meticulously crafted proposal, one that not only redefined ThermaDynamics' business model but had the potential to transform the entire industry.

By the time the presentation was finalized, they knew they weren't just pitching a new idea. Instead, they were challenging the board to see AI and sustainability in a completely new light; Intelligent Cooling-as-a-Service wasn't just a strategy, it was the future.

> **Business Case: Intelligent Cooling-as-a-Service (ICaaS) Model**
> **Presented to:** Board of Directors
> **Prepared by:** Vikram Mehta, Elena Navarro, and Serge Closer

Overview

ThermaDynamics proposes a strategic shift towards providing climate management as a service. For select segments - particularly in emerging markets where customers often have limited purchasing power - we offer an alternative to the traditional model of buying high-efficiency but expensive cooling systems. Instead, we install these systems at no upfront cost and charge a monthly subscription fee for maintaining a stable indoor temperature, supported by a tailored go-to-market approach designed to address the unique needs of these regions.

This Intelligent Cooling-as-a-Service (ICaaS) model moves us from solely being a hardware manufacturer to being a manufacturer and a climate solutions provider, creating:

- A steady, subscription-based revenue stream to compensate for the volatility of one-time sales.
- Stronger customer relationships through ongoing service and data-driven efficiency.
- A scalable model that enables underserved businesses and communities to access premium, AI-powered cooling.
- Increased sustainability impact, aligning energy efficiency with financial incentives.

By leveraging AI to optimize temperature control and energy efficiency, this model not only increases profitability but also drives sustainability at scale.

How It Works

- No upfront cost for customers - Businesses, institutions, and underserved communities receive our high-efficiency AI-powered cooling systems for free.
- ThermaDynamics manages the system - AI optimizes cooling cycles, reduces energy waste, predicts maintenance needs, and adjusts dynamically based on external factors.
- Customers pay for outcomes, not equipment - A fixed monthly fee guarantees a stable indoor temperature (e.g., 22°C) rather than fluctuating energy costs.
- Profitability is driven by AI efficiency - The less energy we use to maintain optimal conditions, the higher our margins.

Key Benefits

1. Recurring Revenue Stream
   - Complements volatile, one-time equipment sales with steady, subscription-based income.
   - Creates predictable, long-term contracts.
2. Market Expansion
   - Removes the upfront financial barrier for businesses, schools, and low-income communities.
   - Makes cutting-edge cooling technology accessible to markets previously priced out.
3. Sustainability at Scale
   - Incentivizes energy efficiency; we maximize savings by reducing unnecessary cooling.
   - Directly reduces carbon footprints in commercial and residential sectors.
4. AI-Driven Cost Savings
   - Optimized energy use lowers operating costs while maintaining customer comfort.
   - Predictive maintenance reduces downtime and expensive repairs.

- Dynamic energy pricing allows the system to shift cooling demand to off-peak hours, cutting expenses.
5. Competitive Differentiation
   - Transforms ThermaDynamics from solely a hardware manufacturer into a smart climate solutions provider.
   - Establishes an AI-powered business model that competitors will struggle to replicate at scale.

Financial Model (Simplified Example)

Scenario	One-Time Sale Model	Subscription Model (ICaaS)
Unit Cost	$5,000 per AC unit	$0 upfront
Revenue per Customer	One-time $5,000	$200/month over 5 years ($12,000)
Margin Control	None (customer operates AC)	Full control (AI optimizes efficiency)
Customer Lock-in	None (one-time sale)	5+ year contracts

Under this model, ThermaDynamics earns 2.4x more revenue over five years while reducing sales friction.

Go-To-Market Strategy
- Pilot Program - Launch a 12-month pilot in selected commercial buildings and underserved communities.
- Strategic Partnerships - Engage with governments, NGOs, and green financing institutions to support initial rollouts.
- Scalability Plan - Expand to global markets, starting with regions experiencing rising temperatures and energy costs.
- AI Efficiency Refinements - Continuously improve predictive models to enhance cost savings and operational efficiency.

Risk Mitigation Strategy
- Managing Upfront Costs - Offset initial investments with financing, government incentives, and strategic leasing agreements.

- Reducing Customer Churn - Multi-year contracts ensure predictable revenue and service continuity.
- Ensuring Operational Efficiency - AI-based temperature control keeps cooling costs below pricing thresholds, preserving margins.
- Predictive Analytics - Minimize maintenance costs and prevent system failures.

Board Decision Request

We request approval to launch a 12-month pilot program in select urban commercial sites and developing communities. The pilot will assess:

- Financial feasibility - Validating the revenue model and long-term profitability.
- Operational scalability - Testing AI optimization and efficiency in different climates.
- Market acceptance - Evaluating customer adoption and long-term retention.

Next Steps Post-Pilot

If successful, we will expand the ICaaS model globally, positioning ThermaDynamics as an industry leader in AI-powered climate management.

This is a rare opportunity to redefine an entire industry, not just improving air conditioning, but reimagining how cooling is delivered, monetized, and sustained for the future.

Chapter 11

CUSTOMER RESISTANCE

Change is easy to promise,
until it asks customers to change, too.

Understanding Market Hesitation

Mehta and Navarro had spent months battling resistance from within. But there was another battlefield they hadn't yet conquered: customers.

Despite the company's efforts, adoption of AI-driven sustainability solutions was not taking off as expected. Sales data showed that while initial client reactions were enthusiastic, actual conversion rates were abysmal. Only 12% of potential buyers had followed through with purchases.

At a strategy meeting, Serge Closer laid it out bluntly. "Our clients don't want to be first. They want to see it in action first. No one wants to risk millions on technology they're not convinced will work at scale."

"Even if it cuts their energy costs by 20%?" Navarro pressed.

"Doesn't matter," Closer replied, shaking his head. "They want proof. And right now, we don't have enough case studies showing measurable success."

Customer Concerns and Feedback

Mehta rubbed his temples. "What exactly are they telling you? We need specifics if we're going to adjust our approach."

Closer nodded and opened his tablet. "I've categorized the main objections. First and most common is the risk of operational disruptions." He turned the tablet to show them a chart. "Nearly seventy percent of potential clients expressed concern that implementing our AI sustainability solutions would interfere with their existing workflows."

"But that's precisely what the pilots were designed to demonstrate; minimal disruption," Navarro objected.

"They don't care about our pilots," Closer continued. "They care about their operations. The manufacturing director at Titan Motors put it bluntly: 'We can't afford even a two percent efficiency drop during implementation when we're running at capacity.'"

Mehta scribbled notes on his pad. "What else?"

"Scalability doubts," Closer replied. "They're skeptical that what worked in our controlled pilot environments will deliver consistent results across their varied facilities and operating conditions." He flipped to another page. "Westbrook Manufacturing has seventeen plants across three continents. Their CTO specifically asked how our system would handle the different equipment generations and local operating procedures."

Navarro nodded slowly. "Fair concern. We haven't tested at that scale yet."

"Third issue, and this is a big one, financial justification." Closer's voice took on the frustrated tone of someone who'd heard the same objection repeatedly. "CFOs and procurement teams want guaranteed ROI data before they'll approve these investments."

"That's impossible," Mehta interjected. "We can provide projections based on our models and pilot data, but guarantees? In untested environments?"

"I know," Closer agreed, "but that's what they're demanding. The CFO at Continental HVAC said, and I quote, 'Show me where three competitors in my space have achieved these returns, and then we can talk.' It's a classic chicken-and-egg situation."

Navarro leaned back in her chair, processing the information. "And the fourth?"

"Lack of industry standards," Closer said. "Several companies, especially the more conservative ones, want validation from industry bodies before they'll commit. They're asking about IEEE or ISO certifications for our AI systems and sustainability metrics."

The room fell silent as they absorbed the feedback. The early optimism that had followed their product pilot successes was evaporating in the face of market hesitation.

Navarro finally broke the silence. "So, we're stuck in the valley of death between innovation and adoption."

"Precisely," Closer nodded. "Everyone's interested, but no one wants to jump first. And with each passing week, the pressure increases."

Mehta stood up and walked to the whiteboard. "We need to segment this problem." He drew a quick matrix. "Which industries and company types are showing the least resistance?"

Closer flipped through his notes. "Smaller companies with visionary leadership are more willing to take risks, but they have limited budgets. Among larger companies, those facing regulatory pressure or with strong public sustainability commitments show more interest."

"And what about specific pain points?" Navarro asked. "Are there particular aspects of our solution that generate more interest than others?"

"Energy cost reduction gets the most attention," Closer replied. "Companies understand that calculation. The sustainability benefits are seen more as PR value than business value, unfortunately."

Mehta nodded as he continued to sketch on the whiteboard. "So, we need to lead with clear financial benefits, address operational disruption fears, demonstrate scalability, and work on industry validation."

Closer closed his folder. "There is one bright spot. The companies that have engaged most seriously with our pilot programs are starting to talk to each other. Word is spreading, slowly but surely." He allowed himself a small smile. "And the positive results are getting harder to ignore."

This was a small opening, a tiny crack in the wall of resistance. It wasn't much, but it was something they could work with.

"We need to adjust our approach," Navarro said decisively. "Focus on specific segments with the largest pain points, where our solution offers the clearest value proposition."

Mehta nodded in agreement. "And we need to build a coalition of early adopters who can validate our results for others."

"The sales team is ready when you are," Closer said, standing up. "But we need something concrete to counter these objections. Something that changes

the conversation."

As Closer left the room, Navarro turned to Mehta. "We need to change perceptions that have been building for years."

Mehta stared at his notes for a long moment before a spark of recognition lit up his eyes. "We're approaching this all wrong. We're telling them what our technology can do instead of showing them what it has done."

"Exactly," Navarro agreed, quickly catching his train of thought. "We need to document every win, every efficiency gain, every dollar saved from our pilot programs."

Mehta began sketching rapidly on the whiteboard. "A complete overhaul of our sales approach. First, detailed case studies with measurable cost reductions and efficiency improvements, hard numbers that CFOs can't dismiss."

"And customer testimonials," Navarro added. "We connect prospects directly with our early adopters. Let them hear about the impact firsthand from someone who isn't trying to sell them anything."

"Live demonstrations," Mehta continued, his marker squeaking across the board. "Not PowerPoints, actual proof. On-site trials customized to their specific challenges."

Navarro was already typing notes into her tablet. "We'll design tailored proof-of-concept sessions that showcase immediate benefits, not theoretical long-term gains."

"Virtual demonstrations for international clients," Mehta added. "Real-time data from existing implementations they can monitor themselves."

They looked at each other, a renewed sense of purpose energizing them both. The path forward was suddenly clearer: not just addressing objections but systematically dismantling them with irrefutable evidence.

"It won't be easy," Navarro cautioned. "We'll need to coordinate with the pilot sites, get legal clearance for the testimonials, and develop custom demonstration packages."

Mehta's expression was determined as he capped his marker. "Then we'd better get started."

As they gathered their materials to leave, both knew that progress in the market would still be hard-won, one customer at a time. But at least now they had a strategy that addressed the core of the resistance, the need for proof before promise.

Scaling Beyond the First Deal

The success of the Riverview Properties deal had proven that the technology worked, but it wasn't enough. ThermaDynamics needed more clients, and fast. The leadership team realized that a single win wouldn't convince the broader market. It needed to create a repeatable sales model that could scale.

The team agreed on a targeted expansion strategy:

- Mid-Sized Industrial Clients: Unlike massive corporations with extensive procurement processes, mid-sized manufacturers had greater agility in decision-making. Targeting them with a low-risk, high-reward pilot program would accelerate adoption.
- Retail and Commercial Buildings: As cities worldwide introduced stricter carbon regulations, shopping centers and office spaces faced

compliance pressure. AI-driven energy optimization was a way to meet mandates while cutting costs.
- Public Sector Contracts: Municipalities and government buildings were actively seeking sustainability solutions to align with climate commitments. ThermaDynamics began lobbying for inclusion in government-backed energy efficiency programs.

Expanding the Pilot Model

Instead of relying on traditional sales approaches, Mehta and Navaro worked with Closer to formalize a three-step customer adoption strategy:
1. No-risk pilot programs: Offer select clients a trial period with no upfront commitment to build trust in AI-driven sustainability solutions. Implement small-scale pilots tailored to each client's operational environment to demonstrate tangible benefits. Collect real-time performance data to show measurable cost savings and efficiency gains. Provide detailed reports at the end of the trial to highlight key takeaways and justify full-scale adoption. Use successful pilot cases as testimonials for future prospects, creating a cycle of market confidence and increased adoption.
2. Industry-specific ROI simulations: Conduct in-depth analysis of various industries to identify unique energy consumption patterns. Develop AI-driven financial models to estimate cost savings for specific business segments. Present data-backed ROI projections to demonstrate how AI optimization directly impacts bottom-line performance. Customize solution presentations for different industries, ensuring relevance to each client's operational needs. Collect and showcase testimonials from early adopters to validate real-world success stories.
3. Competitive benchmarking: Identify and analyze competitors implementing AI-driven sustainability solutions. Gather case studies showcasing measurable improvements in energy efficiency and cost reductions. Highlight industry leaders already investing in AI to create urgency among hesitant clients. Develop side-by-side comparisons of ThermaDynamics' solutions versus competitors to emphasize unique advantages. Use market trend reports to demonstrate the inevitability of AI adoption in sustainability efforts.

Within three months, the shift in strategy led to remarkable results. Inbound client inquiries surged by 52%, reflecting growing interest in AI-driven sustainability solutions. Conversion rates climbed from 12% to 38%, demonstrating that potential buyers were no longer just curious, they were committing. The strategy also secured three high-profile contracts spanning manufacturing, commercial real estate, and government sectors, generating over $50 million in revenue. This newfound momentum solidified ThermaDynamics' credibility, proving that AI-powered sustainability was not just a vision, but a profitable and scalable reality.

A New Market Reputation

The twin transformation was no longer seen as an unproven experiment; it was now a rising leader in AI-driven sustainability. Competitors who had initially dismissed the company's pivot were scrambling to catch up, and industry analysts began recognizing ThermaDynamics as a serious player in smart building solutions.

Additionally, early adopters provided public endorsements, strengthening the company's credibility. Reports from satisfied clients highlighted benefits such as:

- Faster ROI than initially projected: Several businesses saw energy cost reductions of up to 25% within the first six months.
- Operational efficiency improvements: AI-driven automation optimized maintenance schedules, reducing equipment downtime by 30%.
- Regulatory compliance made easier: Clients successfully met new carbon footprint regulations without costly retrofits.

At the end of the quarter, Mehta and Navarro reviewed the numbers. "We finally have traction."

100

Chapter 12

THE BOARD'S ULTIMATUM

Every transformation reaches a moment
when belief must turn into results, or retreat.

Mounting Pressure from the Board

Despite the breakthrough with Riverview Properties and other high-profile contracts, internal opposition to the twin transformation initiative was intensifying. Richard Steele was leading the charge against it, using ThermaDynamics' recent market struggles as ammunition.

At a tense board meeting, Steele slammed a report on the conference table. "We continue to lose market share to Chinese competitors," he stated, his voice sharp. "And what's our response? Experimental projects that drain resources without guaranteed returns."

The room remained silent, executives exchanging uneasy glances. Thomas Greaves sat at the head of the table, hands clasped in front of him, his expression inscrutable. Steele continued, his frustration mounting.

"This is a war for survival, not a playground for experiments," he declared. "We need to focus on core business stability, our tried-and-tested products, not some unproven AI initiative that's eating up resources and distracting from real revenue generation."

Greaves shifted in his seat, and when he spoke, his voice was firm. "We're not running experiments, Richard. We're adapting. AI-driven efficiency isn't up for debate anymore; you've seen the numbers. Our early results prove it can cut costs, optimize production, and increase operational agility. Plus, you can see the new sales numbers. That's why we put forward the new business model."

Steele bristled, flipping through the executive summary of the twin transformation initiative. "I buy AI as a tool for cost-cutting and efficiency. Customers seem to like it. But sustainability?" He shook his head. "That's still a gamble. I don't think it drives revenue and I don't think customers really care. We're not running a charity."

Other board members murmured in agreement. AI had won its place at the table, but sustainability was still viewed as a luxury, one that needed to justify its worth in hard numbers. Greaves sighed, knowing this was the best deal they were going to get.

"Fair enough," he said. "Give us six months. If we don't show profitability, we'll reassess."

Steele nodded, satisfied for now. "Six months. No more."

The meeting adjourned, but the message was clear: sustainability had to prove itself, and fast.

The CEO's Ultimatum

After the meeting, Greaves called Mehta and Navarro into his office. The heavy oak door shut behind them, sealing them in a room that suddenly felt uncomfortably small. His usually composed demeanor was visibly strained as he gestured for them to sit down.

"I'm going to be blunt," Greaves said, his voice lower than usual. "You have six months to deliver concrete, company-wide results, or the twin transformation is dead."

Navarro's stomach dropped. Mehta frowned, his mind already racing.

Greaves rubbed his temples before continuing. "The board is demanding we refocus on regaining market share. If we can't prove that this initiative is a profit driver, I won't have the leverage to protect it anymore."

Mehta finally spoke, his voice steady but edged with tension. "We've just secured our first major clients, and the results are tracking positively. The data is there, we just need time to scale."

"Time is a luxury I don't have," Greaves sighed. His voice carried the weight of months of mounting pressure. "I need immediate, undeniable wins.

You need to expand beyond pilots and show measurable success: revenue growth, cost savings, and operational efficiency."

Navarro glanced at Mehta before answering. "If we can scale quickly, prove savings across multiple factories, and lock in new customers, will that be enough to hold off the board?"

Greaves hesitated. "Let's put it this way. If you can cut company-wide operational costs by at least 10%, bring in two more major clients, and show a hard financial impact within six months, I might be able to keep Steele and his allies at bay. But anything less, and the initiative dies."

The silence in the room felt suffocating.

A Race Against Time

Navarro and Mehta left Greaves' office with the grim realization that they needed a rapid, company-wide rollout plan, one that delivered immediate financial impact while also proving long-term viability.

They had to think bigger.

Instead of focusing primarily on external sales, they would double down on internal efficiencies, targeting factory-wide AI optimization, procurement cost reductions, and predictive maintenance integration.

Within a week, Mehta and Navarro gathered leaders from operations, finance, IT, and sales for a project review. The tension in the air was palpable as they laid out their plan.

"The board won't wait for long-term gains," Mehta stated. "We need results within months."

Navarro added, her tone urgent, "We'll prioritize low-hanging fruit, like energy cost reductions, quick-turn AI efficiency boosts, and supply chain streamlining. These need to be visible wins."

Fred LaPlante, the COO, leaned back in his chair, arms crossed. "You really think you can roll out AI across the company and make it profitable in six months? I've been in this business for thirty years. Nothing happens that fast."

Navarro met his gaze head-on. "Then maybe it's time we change how things happen."

LaPlante snorted. "I'll believe it when I see it."

Meanwhile, CFO Katarina Svensson remained doubtful. She flipped through the financial projections. "If I'm signing off on these investments, I need an ROI breakdown with actual numbers. No assumptions, no best-case scenarios."

Mehta nodded. "We'll give you a monthly report with full transparency, down to the cent. But we need your backing to move forward at scale."

Svensson sighed, putting down the report. "I'm not saying no. But I'm not giving you a blank check, either. Show me the numbers as they come in."

The War Room Strategy

Knowing that the next six months would determine the future of the twin transformation at ThermaDynamics, Mehta and Navarro transformed an executive conference room into a fully functional war room. Whiteboards lined the walls, covered in aggressive timelines, financial projections, and target factory lists. A real-time dashboard displayed energy consumption data and pilot results, ensuring immediate visibility into key performance metrics.

They divided responsibilities into task forces:

- Factory optimization team: Tasked with rolling out AI across three additional facilities, focusing on cutting energy waste by 10-15% per site.
- Supply chain analytics team: Dedicated to implementing AI-driven procurement strategies to achieve $15 million in cost reductions within the first quarter.
- Predictive maintenance task force: Focused on reducing equipment downtime by 25% through advanced AI monitoring.
- Sales expansion team: Charged with securing two additional major clients willing to implement AI-powered energy management solutions.
- ICaaS (Intelligent Cooling-as-a-Service) implementation team: Responsible for launching the ICaaS pilot.

Daily stand-up meetings kept everyone aligned, and a dedicated response team handled operational roadblocks in real time. The objective was clear: demonstrate undeniable value, fast.

As Mehta and Navarro surveyed the room, they felt the magnitude of the task ahead. The strategy was in place. Now, execution was all that mattered.

Navarro crossed her arms. "This is it. We either prove this works, or we're done."

Mehta nodded. "Then let's get to work."

Transformation Takeaways: Memo to Leadership

To: Thomas Greaves, CEO

From: Elena Navarro, Chief Sustainability Officer, and Vikram Mehta, Chief AI Officer

Date: June 2026

Subject: Lessons from Early Challenges in the Twin Transformation

✓ What Worked

- **Start with Scope 1 for focus and credibility.**
  Concentrating on direct emissions (Scope 1) allowed the team to generate quick wins, build internal trust, and prove the business case before expanding into more complex Scope 2 and 3 challenges.
- **Reframed sustainability as a performance driver.**
  Positioned sustainability not as a cost center but as a source of operational efficiency, cost reduction, and market differentiation, gaining traction with skeptical stakeholders.
- **Digital twins and edge AI provided real-time insight and agility.**
  Leveraging digital twin technology and edge AI enabled high-impact simulations and fast, localized decision-making, which improved both system performance and energy efficiency.
- **Breakthroughs came from open innovation.**
  Inviting outside experts and customers to contribute to product design and optimization led to faster innovation and deeper engagement, unlocking customer-facing opportunities and new revenue streams.
- **Pivoting to product-focused sustainability opened market doors.**
  Shifting the focus from internal operations to customer energy savings (e.g., smart HVAC systems) gave sales teams a compelling story to tell and generated demand-side momentum.

✗ What Didn't Work

- **Premature rollout without cultural groundwork created resistance.**
  The AI pilot in Texas triggered worker suspicion and mid-manager backlash due to inadequate communication and lack of human-centered change management.
- **Initial over-reliance on technical performance over human buy-in.**
  Early focus on simulations and technical precision overlooked the need for frontline trust, leading to productivity drops, overridden recommendations, and avoidable downtime.
- **Sustainability still lacked legitimacy with some board members.**
  Despite operational progress, several board members continued to see sustainability as a soft priority, disconnected from revenue and strategic risk.
- **Customer adoption stalled due to lack of proof and standards.**
  Many clients were interested in ThermaDynamics' AI-powered offerings but delayed adoption due to perceived risks, unproven scalability, and absence of third-party validation.
- **Early internal success failed to translate into market confidence.**
  Despite positive internal metrics, external buyers demanded third-party benchmarks, peer case studies, and industry certification—none of which were in place at first.

📖 Lessons Learned

- **Begin with controllable variables to establish credibility.**
  Tackle Scope 1 emissions and internal optimization before venturing into externally dependent areas. Small wins in familiar territory are essential to prove feasibility.
- **Reposition sustainability as a business performance lever, not a moral imperative.**

Sustainability efforts gained momentum when framed as cost savings, operational efficiency, and customer retention, not as a standalone moral goal.

- **Operational transformation requires cultural transformation.** No AI system will succeed without trust from the humans it supports. Change management, transparency, and training must be embedded from day one.
- **Technological change must be phased and human-centric.** Start with low-risk applications and allow workers to override or shape AI recommendations to build confidence.
- **Market adoption hinges on validation, not just innovation.** Early client wins must be documented in detail. Peer testimonials, ROI figures, and standards alignment turn interest into action.
- **Cross-industry learning accelerates innovation.** Borrowing proven solutions from adjacent industries unlocks faster breakthroughs than internal development alone. Innovation doesn't have to start from scratch.
- **Hybrid AI architectures maximize speed and efficiency.** Edge computing ensures rapid, real-time optimization while centralized cloud systems power simulations and strategic decisions. Combining both is key.
- **Business model innovation is a force multiplier.** Transitioning from product sales to AI-powered service offerings aligned financial incentives with sustainability, created recurring revenue, and opened new markets.

Elena & Vikram

ACT 3

TURNING THE TIDE

Chapter 13

THE PUSH FOR QUICK WINS

In a skeptical system,
momentum is the most persuasive argument.

The CFO's Reluctant Approval

Mehta and Navarro knew that if they had any chance of keeping the twin transformation initiative alive, they needed fast, measurable success. The board's pressure was mounting, and the six-month deadline loomed over them like a storm cloud. Their best bet? A small, controlled rollout that could deliver undeniable cost savings.

They scheduled a meeting with CFO Katarina Svensson, the gatekeeper of all financial approvals. Svensson was notorious for her demand for hard evidence before greenlighting any investment. If they couldn't convince her, the initiative was doomed before it had a chance to scale.

Mehta, armed with data from their pilot programs, took the lead. "Katarina, we're proposing a limited rollout of AI-driven energy optimization at our largest production facility in Texas. The numbers from the pilot project suggest that we can cut energy costs by at least 15% within the first three months, and potentially by 20% within six months."

Svensson leaned back in her chair, her gaze steady and assessing. "Projected savings aren't actual savings, Vikram. We both know that. What's the worst-case scenario here? I need to know the risks."

Navarro maintained an air of composed determination. "The absolute worst-case scenario is that we don't reach our full optimization potential, but we will still see at least a 10% reduction in costs, which translates to $5 million in annual savings for just this one factory. And since we're proposing an incremental approach, the initial investment is minimal: $500,000 to deploy and integrate the AI system. If we don't hit the targets within six months, we shut it down. No further commitment."

Svensson's lips pressed into a thin line as she considered the numbers. "And if it fails completely? If something goes wrong with the system?"

Mehta was ready. "That's why we're working closely with IT and Operations to ensure that any implementation hiccups don't affect productivity. If the AI malfunctions, we have immediate rollback capabilities. There's virtually no risk to our production schedules."

Svensson sighed, drumming her fingers on the desk. "Fine. I'll approve the funds for the rollout in Texas," she finally said. "But I want regular reports with real, quantifiable data. If we don't see significant progress, we pull the plug."

Mehta and Navarro looked at each other, a flicker of victory passing between them. Step one was complete.

Rolling Out the Trial

With Svensson's reluctant approval, Mehta and Navarro wasted no time. They worked closely with the operations team and IT department to deploy the AI-driven energy management system at the Texas factory. The system leveraged real-time data analytics and predictive algorithms to optimize power consumption, reduce energy waste, and adjust equipment loads based on production schedules.

But cooperation with IT was anything but smooth. The department, already wary of Mehta's growing influence, dragged its heels on key deliverables, citing security concerns and protocol reviews that seemed to materialize out of nowhere. Access to critical data sources was delayed without explanation, and integration requests were met with bureaucratic pushback. At one point, Mehta's team had to escalate an issue all the way to Greaves just to gain read/write permissions on factory telemetry logs.

It quickly became clear that this wasn't just about technical compatibility, it was political. Maria Fernandes, as CIO, had yet to publicly oppose the project, but her team's passive resistance was unmistakable. Every small win came at the cost of time, energy, and negotiation.

The early days were also fraught with obstacles on the factory floor. Some workers resisted the new AI systems, fearing automation would lead to job losses. Others simply didn't trust the technology.

"What happens when this thing tells us to shut down a line mid-shift?" one factory supervisor asked during a training session.

"It won't," Mehta assured him. "The AI is designed to adapt to production schedules, not disrupt them. It's not making decisions on its own. It's giving you better information so you can make the smartest decision."

"I'll believe it when I see it," the supervisor muttered, his expression grim.

Within weeks, initial results started trickling in:

- Energy waste dropped by 12% in the first month alone.
- By the end of the second month, total energy costs had fallen by 18%.
- After three months, they had reached a full 20% reduction in energy expenses, resulting in $1.2 million in savings.

The Skeptics Remain

Despite the strong early results, however, the skeptics remained unconvinced.

Fred LaPlante, the COO, was quick to dismiss the findings. "This is one factory. We operate in a global network with vastly different infrastructures. What works in Texas might not work in China or Europe. Scaling this isn't as simple as copying and pasting data models."

Richard Steele, the Board Chairman, was equally unimpressed. "Even if we grant that this can reduce costs in the short term, how does this help us regain market share? We're still losing ground to competitors and cutting energy costs doesn't sell more products."

Mehta's patience was wearing thin. "It does, actually," he said, his voice sharper than usual. "Lower costs mean we increase our margins without raising prices. It allows us to invest in R&D for next-generation smart-building solutions. This is something that differentiates us from the competition."

Steele gestured dismissively. "That's a long-term play. We need immediate, revenue-driving strategies."

Navarro refused to back down. "You want an immediate win?" she asked. "Then we take this data and use it as a selling point. Show customers that our factories are more efficient, more sustainable, and more cost-effective than our competitors'. That builds brand loyalty, attracts eco-conscious clients, and reduces the prices of our products."

Steele reflected for a minute. "You might have a point."

A Partial Victory, But the Battle Continues

Despite their best efforts, however, the board refused to approve a full-scale rollout. Instead, they granted a second trial at a European facility, agreeing to reassess after another quarter of data collection. The decision was frustrating, but it kept the initiative alive, for now.

As Mehta and Navarro left the boardroom, Navarro muttered, "We need a game-changer. Something that forces their hand."

Chapter 14

THE PUBLIC RELATIONS SETBACK

In transformation, perception can outpace progress, or poison it.

The Leak That Shook the Company

ThermaDynamics' twin transformation initiative had started to gain traction. With promising early results from the pilot projects and tentative board approval for further trials, Mehta and Navarro had begun to believe they could turn the tide in their favor. But just as momentum was building, disaster struck.

A confidential sustainability report surfaced in the media, alleging that ThermaDynamics had exaggerated its environmental impact reductions. The report, supposedly compiled by an independent watchdog group, claimed that the company's AI-driven energy optimizations had only led to a 5-7% reduction in emissions, far below the 20% figure they had been publicly promoting. Worse, it suggested that the company had failed to account for emissions generated during the manufacturing of its new smart-energy systems, negating much of the perceived progress.

The backlash was immediate and unforgiving. Industry publications dissected the report, questioning the integrity of ThermaDynamics' claims. Social media platforms exploded with criticism, and sustainability influencers called the company's green commitments a marketing ploy. Hashtags like

#GreenwashingTherma and #SustainabilityScam trended overnight. Customers who had begun considering ThermaDynamics' AI-powered solutions were now hesitating, fearful of reputational damage by association.

Financial analysts and investment firms took notice. Several issued downgraded stock ratings, citing potential regulatory scrutiny and consumer distrust. Within 72 hours of the leak, ThermaDynamics' stock price had dropped 8%, wiping millions from its market capitalization. Investors flooded the company's communications team with questions, demanding an explanation.

Richard Steele Seizes the Moment

At an emergency board meeting, Richard Steele wasted no time in leveraging the crisis to undermine Mehta and Navarro's initiative.

"This," he said, waving a printed copy of the leaked report, "is exactly why we don't gamble with unproven initiatives. This isn't just a bad news cycle. It's a credibility catastrophe. Our customers, and our core industrial partners, value one thing above all: reliability. And right now, we're anything but reliable."

Navarro clenched her fists under the table. "With all due respect, Richard, the report is misleading. It selectively omits data from our AI optimization trials that show long-term benefits. This isn't about deception, it's about the methodology they used to measure results."

Steele huffed. "Public perception is reality, Elena. If they believe we're misleading them, then we are. You can't PR-spin your way out of numbers that don't add up."

Fred LaPlante jumped in, his voice laced with frustration. "This is why I've been against this from the beginning. We've poured millions into this initiative, and what do we have to show for it? A PR disaster, shaky data, and a loss of investor confidence. We should be focusing on what we do best: manufacturing high-performance, high-reliability products. Not chasing media narratives."

Navarro looked toward Katarina Svensson, the CFO, hoping for support, but she merely folded her hands. "We have a bigger problem than PR," Svensson said carefully. "Major clients are reconsidering their contracts. We've received emails from three Fortune 500 partners asking for reassurances that our sustainability numbers are legitimate before they finalize any new orders."

Internal Divisions Deepen

The divide within the company had never been starker. Steele and LaPlante were advocating for a damage-control strategy, urging the company to pull back from twin transformation messaging and return to a focus on cost-efficiency and product reliability. On the other side, Mehta and Navarro were fighting to defend the initiative, arguing that abandoning it would only validate critics' claims that ThermaDynamics had something to hide.

Mehta, keeping his voice measured, spoke up. "This isn't just about sustainability. Our AI-driven optimizations are saving money. We've already seen a 20% reduction in energy costs in our Texas factory. Those savings are real, tangible, and scalable."

Steele didn't budge. "Energy savings don't mean a damn thing if our biggest customers no longer trust us. Every business we deal with has sustainability goals now, and if they think we're falsifying numbers, they'll distance themselves from us."

Svensson nodded. "Our marketing team is already seeing declining engagement on our latest campaigns. The backlash is spreading beyond niche sustainability circles. The last thing we need is a shareholder revolt."

The Fight for Control

Navarro turned to the Greaves, who had remained mostly silent. "Thomas, this initiative is about more than just our reputation. It's about staying ahead in a market that's shifting towards AI-driven efficiency. If we backtrack now, we'll be seen as not just dishonest, but as incapable of innovation."

Greaves sighed heavily. "I don't disagree with you, Elena, but the reality is we're hemorrhaging trust. If we don't stabilize investor confidence, this could spiral into something much worse."

Steele saw his opportunity. "Then let's make the hard decision. Halt the twin transformation. We go back to core fundamentals, reinforce trust in our traditional operations, and rebuild credibility the right way."

Mehta's jaw tightened. "So, you want us to retreat at the first sign of resistance?"

"No," Steele said coolly, "I want us to stop setting ourselves up for failure."

A heavy silence followed. The weight of the decision loomed over them. Finally, Greaves straightened in his chair. "Here's what we're going to do," he said. "We'll launch an internal audit of our sustainability numbers. We'll bring in third-party verification to validate our claims. If they confirm our data, we'll push back against the watchdog report and defend our progress."

"And if they don't?" Svensson asked.

Greaves hesitated. "Then we reassess."

After Steele and the others had left, Mehta and Navarro remained with Greaves.

"I don't need to tell you how serious this is," Greaves said quietly. "This isn't just an internal battle anymore. The regulators have the power to validate or invalidate everything we've worked for."

Navarro nodded. "This could get even worse. The EU Carbon Trust certification review is next month. Without that certification, we lose access to government contracts across Europe that make up 22% of our projected growth for next year."

"We'l need to open our data completely," Mehta said. "Show them our methodology, our raw measurements, everything. At least we have access to all the data."

"Let's get the Texas facility ready for inspection," Navarro added. "They'll want to see our systems in action, verify that real emissions reductions are happening as we claim."

As they left the boardroom, the gravity of the situation was clear to them. The pressure was no longer just from the board. It came from external regulators with the power to determine whether ThermaDynamics' sustainability transformation was legitimate, and with it, the company's access to crucial markets.

Chapter 15

CRISIS OF CONFIDENCE

Doubt is contagious. So is conviction.

Leadership Under Question

The door to the executive conference room closed with a soft click, leaving Greaves and Steele alone with the afternoon sunlight streaming through the floor-to-ceiling windows. The boardroom table that normally hosted twelve now held only two, the emptiness amplifying the tension between them.

"The market has lost confidence in us, Thomas," Steele said, his voice low yet insistent. "We have clients delaying contracts. Investors want to know why we're leaning so heavily on unproven systems that appear to have major flaws. And more importantly..." he paused, looking up at Greaves, "they want to know if we have the right leadership to fix this."

Greaves shook his head in disagreement. "We expected resistance to change. We expected challenges along the way. What we didn't expect was just how successful the twin transformation would become before the controversy hit."

He gestured to a set of documents in front of him. "Despite the PR crisis, our twin transformation initiatives have cut operational waste by 19%, dropped energy costs by 22%, and increased productivity across our factories. You think the market has lost confidence in us? Look at the clients who haven't cancelled contracts. Look at the ones signing extensions."

Steele's expression hardened. "And what about the reports showing our sustainability impact might have been exaggerated?"

Greaves met his gaze evenly. "We fix them. That's what this company does. When our early computerized control systems malfunctioned in the '90s, did we scrap them? No. We improved them. When we introduced automated assembly and factory workers fought it, did we abandon it? No. We proved to them it would make their jobs better." He looked around. "That's what this moment is. A challenge to overcome. Not a reason to reverse course."

Steele leaned back, his expression unreadable. "Patricia Wong called me yesterday. She thinks the full board needs to discuss whether your leadership is still suited for this moment." He delivered the statement flatly, watching Greaves' reaction. "Her words, not mine."

Greaves stiffened imperceptibly. "And what did you tell her?"

"That I'd speak with you first." Steele stood up from his chair and moved to the window, gazing out at the campus below. "It's no surprise that James Morrison agrees with her. Says this company can't afford more reputational hits." He turned back to face Greaves. "And who's to say this won't happen again? Even if we fix the current mess, this technology is moving too fast. Investors need stability."

The subtext was clear. This wasn't just a discussion about AI and sustainability; it was about Greaves. His role. His future.

Greaves leaned forward in his chair. "If they want stability, they can go back to the old model. Stick with what's safe. But in five years, this company won't be a market leader anymore. It will be playing catch-up to competitors that took the risks we didn't."

Silence filled the room.

"I don't disagree that change is necessary, Thomas." Steele's tone was different now, less aggressive, more conciliatory. "But the board has a responsibility to make sure we have the right leadership for it."

Greaves recognized the threat. After decades with the company, the last ten as CEO, his position wasn't as secure as he'd once believed.

"The clients who are nervous about AI right now," Greaves said carefully, "are the same ones who demanded we become more sustainable in the first place. This transformation wasn't optional; it was a necessity. We fix the technical issues, we rebuild trust, and we keep moving forward."

The tension in the room shifted subtly.

Finally, Steele turned around and looked directly at Greaves. "I'll hold back Wong and Morrison for now. But let me be clear - if this company takes another major hit, our conversation won't be about whether AI and sustainability are worth pursuing. It'll be about who's leading it."

The message couldn't have been clearer. Greaves had won a temporary reprieve, but only barely.

As Steele gathered his papers and prepared to leave, Greaves walked to the window, looking out over the factory campus where he'd spent almost all of his professional life. He didn't turn when he heard Steele pause at the door.

"You weren't really going to push for my removal, were you, Richard?"

Steele was quiet for a moment. "I needed to know if you still believed in this as much as you did a year ago."

Greaves turned to face his mentor, the man who had hired him as a young engineer and who now held his fate in his hands. "And?"

A ghost of a smile crossed Steele's face. "The board meets next week. Make it count, Thomas."

The door closed behind him, leaving Greaves alone with his thoughts.

Chapter 16

WINNING THE WORKFORCE

No system changes until its people believe they have a stake in the future.

The Audit Clears the Air

In a rare stroke of good news, the independent audit that Greaves had ordered delivered a positive verdict. A third-party verification team confirmed that ThermaDynamics' AI-driven energy optimization was achieving its stated results, with a 19.5% reduction in emissions and an 18% decrease in energy costs in test environments. While the watchdog group's initial report had not been entirely inaccurate, it had failed to account for dynamic efficiency improvements that AI provided over time.

Navarro wasted no time in presenting the findings to the rest of the management team. "This is proof that our initiative is not only legitimate, but a strategic advantage. If we continue to refine these models, we could push cost savings even higher while keeping our sustainability commitments intact."

LaPlante, to the surprise of no one, remained dubious. "Numbers on a report don't rebuild trust overnight. Investors and customers still have perception issues about our credibility."

Fernandes seized the opening. "And before we go charging ahead with any new data integrations or tech rollouts, let's remember, we need to pass everything through the IT Steering Board first. That's the process. It's there to reduce risk and ensure alignment."

Svensson, while more open to discussion, was also still cautious. "If we continue forward, we need a strategy to ensure internal alignment and external communication. We can't afford another PR crisis."

Greaves nodded. "Agreed. But this is a chance to regain our footing. I want to see a plan to win over our internal teams first before we expand any further."

Saskia Schmidt Steps In

That's when Saskia Schmidt, ThermaDynamics' Head of HR, stepped in. She had been following the internal tensions and saw the real problem: the workforce didn't trust the AI systems.

"Vikram, Elena," she said after the meeting, "your initiative won't succeed if the people running our factories don't buy in. Right now, they see AI as a threat, not a tool. If you want this to work, you need to change that perception."

Mehta sighed. "We've tried. They push back. They think AI means job cuts and automation replacing their roles."

Schmidt shook her head. "That's because you're telling them how AI helps the company, not how it helps them. We need to flip the script. Let me help."

Engaging the Workforce

With Schmidt's guidance, Mehta and Navarro shifted their focus. Instead of introducing AI as a top-down push for efficiency or cost reduction, they rebranded it as a workforce empowerment strategy. They realized that trust in technology wouldn't come from technical specs alone, it needed to come from people seeing how AI could make their daily work better, not just faster.

They built their communication around a central theme. AI, they emphasized, wasn't here to monitor or replace workers, it was here to take the friction out of the workday: to predict problems before they happened, simplify decisions, and help people focus on what mattered most.

Instead of issuing memos, they turned the spotlight on early users like machine operators, technicians, and line supervisors who could speak credibly about how the AI had helped them in real, practical ways. These stories became a subtle but powerful message: this technology is already part of the team.

One challenge they anticipated, and quickly encountered, was a kind of cultural hesitation: some employees viewed reliance on AI tools as cutting corners, or questioned whether automation would devalue their experience. Schmidt referred to this privately as 'the pride problem'—not resistance to change, but resistance to feeling sidelined.

They addressed it with care. First, by shifting the narrative: using AI wasn't about doing less, it was about doing smarter, safer work. Second, by making it clear that the AI systems weren't decision-makers - they were early warning systems, optimization engines, or assistive tools. Final decisions always stayed with the people on the ground.

To ensure broad acceptance, all workforce training was led and coordinated by HR, with close input from the AI and sustainability teams. By positioning HR as the face of the initiative, the company grounded the training in familiar channels of trust and support.

To support adoption and build momentum, the team introduced several key changes:

1. Hands-on AI workshops: Rather than passive training, they ran live, role-specific workshops. Employees learned how to interpret AI generated alerts, understand predictive models for equipment failures, and use visual dashboards to plan maintenance before issues escalated. The focus wasn't on using new software, it was on building confidence in the insights AI provided.
2. Job security reassurance: AI inevitably led to some processes becoming more efficient, but no jobs were cut. HR introduced a cross-skilling program, helping employees move into adjacent roles where their domain knowledge remained valuable. The message was consistent: your role is evolving, not disappearing.
3. Incentive structures: The company introduced performance bonuses tied to operational improvements where AI played a role, things like reduced downtime, energy savings, or quality consistency. This helped employees see themselves as collaborators in AI-driven success, not just observers of it.

4. AI transparency: Employees gained access to shared dashboards that showed how AI was helping across the board, from detecting early wear in machines to balancing energy usage. This visibility helped demystify the systems and built trust through shared understanding, not just management reports.
5. Peer support champions: Rather than relying solely on formal trainers, the team appointed internal 'AI Champions', frontline employees trained to support their peers. These champions hosted quick drop-in sessions, helped interpret AI alerts, and acted as informal bridges between engineering and operations. HR in collaboration with Mehta and Navarro identified and supported these champions, ensuring that participation was seen as a development opportunity rather than a tech assignment.
6. Monitoring engagement quietly: When certain systems weren't being used as expected 2-3 months post-rollout, the team took a quiet, observational approach, following up with supervisors, tweaking dashboards for usability, and re-engaging teams with tailored follow-up. Rather than enforcement, they leaned on curiosity: what's not working, and why?
7. Onboarding reworked for relevance: Initial onboarding was simplified, using examples from each facility's real data and cases. Instead of abstract theory, training focused on: here's how AI helped in a plant just like yours. Contextual relevance proved more powerful than technical detail.
8. A culture of shared learning: Informal communities started forming around AI use cases, groups of operators sharing insights, maintenance leads comparing alert patterns, and plant managers benchmarking results. The team supported these efforts, but didn't over-engineer them. Peer curiosity did more to accelerate adoption than any formal program could.

By blending practical tools with psychological safety, Mehta and Navarro helped employees move from being doubters to engagers. AI was no longer an abstract system running in the background. It became a quiet partner -

amplifying experience, reducing guesswork, and, most importantly, giving people the confidence to act early rather than react late.

A Shift in Perception

Saskia Schmidt had just concluded her pitch 'demonstrate the practical benefits' to a group of workers when Randy Russo, known among his peers as 'Gearhead,' took his stance. The veteran operator from the Texas plant leaned against a workbench, his oil-stained overalls fitting like a second skin, and waved a dismissive hand at the AI dashboard illuminating the wall.

"Overcomplicated nonsense," he said, his rough voice cutting through the ambient noise, shaped by two decades of managing machinery. "I've kept this production line running since these technicians were children and I don't need an automated system telling me how to do my job."

His crew chuckled and nodded in agreement. Randy was their unofficial spokesperson, voicing doubts at every 'Hands-on AI' workshop. He was pivotal to the operation, and his resistance risked undermining the entire initiative.

Days later, the plant hummed with a different cadence. Midnight had arrived abruptly, orders were piling up, and the line was under strain, when a compressor began to shudder, endangering the entire shift. Randy, wrench in hand, muttered his frustration at the machine until the dashboard flashed red: FAILURE IMMINENT, 10 MINUTES.

"Ridiculous," he grumbled, though he hesitated. Five minutes later, the AI intervened, shutting off power and redirecting airflow. The rattling stopped, replaced by calm. No breakdown, just quiet. "It saved my night, that clever device," he admitted under his breath, a faint smile breaking through as the crew exchanged approving looks. Randy, the most steadfast skeptic, had relented. "I'm not fully convinced," he added, "but it proved its worth." By the end of the shift, efficiency improved by 9%, and even the plant manager, lingering behind, conceded, "If Randy approves, I'll pay attention."

Gradually, the opposition began to dissipate.

The Factory Visit

To gauge the impact of their efforts firsthand, Mehta and Navarro visited the Texas plant, where resistance to AI had initially been strong. As they stepped into the production facility, the hum of machines filled the air, interspersed with conversations among workers gathered around AI-assisted control panels.

A veteran machine operator approached them. As he greeted them, there was no hostility in his expression, only curiosity. "Gotta admit," he said, nodding toward the dashboard displaying real-time equipment performance, "when you guys first brought in AI, I thought it was going to replace us. But now, I'm actually using it to make my shift less stressful. Instead of guessing when a machine's going to fail, now we know. Makes a hell of a difference."

Mehta smiled. "That's exactly what we hoped for. Less guesswork, more control."

Another worker chimed in. "I used to spend half my shift running from one malfunction to another. Now, I get an alert before anything goes wrong. It's saving me a ton of frustration."

Navarro gestured toward the display, where energy consumption metrics were shown in real time. "What about this? Are you seeing any impact?"

The worker nodded. "Yeah. We used to run everything at full capacity all the time. Now, AI helps adjust power use without affecting production. Saves energy, keeps the machines running smoother. And I heard from the maintenance guys that breakdowns are already down by nearly 20%."

LaPlante Takes Notice

Even Fred LaPlante, the COO, who had been one of the biggest doubters, acknowledged the impact. He had initially refused to attend the visit, but after seeing the latest performance reports, he decided to join Mehta and Navarro for a factory walk-through.

"I didn't think you could turn around factory floor sentiment like this," he admitted. "I still have my concerns, but if AI really does keep our machines running longer and our workers more productive, I'm open to seeing how far we can take it."

Navarro seized the moment. "Fred, imagine if we scale this across all facilities. We could be looking at hundreds of millions in operational savings over the next five years."

He nodded slowly. "I'm not saying I'm sold, but... I'm listening."

With internal buy-in improving, Mehta and Navarro prepared for the next stage: scaling the initiative beyond a few select factories. But even as they gained traction within ThermaDynamics, external pressures loomed. Would customers and investors recognize the shift? Or would they still see the company as a damaged brand with unfulfilled promises?

Chapter 17

THE POWER STRUGGLE

Transformation threatens power,
and power rarely goes quietly.

The Battle for AI Control

Just as Mehta and Navarro were beginning to gain momentum, a familiar challenge emerged, one that came from within the company itself. The Chief Information Officer, Maria Fernandes, had her sights set on AI.

At an executive leadership meeting, Fernandes made her move. "ThermaDynamics needs a centralized approach to technology management," she stated in her no-nonsense manner. "AI falls under IT. It should be managed within my department to ensure consistency, security, and alignment with company-wide infrastructure."

Mehta was not surprised. In fact, he had anticipated this move. Fernandes had always been territorial when it came to technology, and now that AI was proving to be a game-changer, she saw an opportunity to consolidate power.

Navarro spoke first. "AI isn't just another IT tool, Maria. It's a business transformation driver. It's fundamentally reshaping how we operate, how we reduce costs, and how we differentiate in the market."

Fernandes softened her tone. "I don't disagree that AI has strategic importance. But allowing it to exist outside of IT governance is a recipe for inefficiencies and security risks. We're already seeing AI deployments scattered across different departments. That's dangerous and inefficient."

Mehta countered. "And what happens when IT buries AI under compliance paperwork, bureaucratic red tape, and outdated policies? AI needs agility to iterate and evolve. We're proving that right now with factory energy optimization, predictive maintenance, and smart-building solutions. None of that happened under IT."

Fernandes' expression didn't change, but her grip on the table tightened. "The problem is that AI is becoming too fragmented within the company. Finance wants AI to cut costs. Sales wants AI to help close deals. Sustainability wants AI to drive green initiatives. If this continues unchecked, we'll have different teams pulling AI in all directions, creating redundancies and unmanageable security risks."

Navarro raised an eyebrow. "And your solution is to centralize AI under IT? That's not coordination, Maria. That's bureaucratic strangulation."

Fernandes' voice grew sharper. "It's governance. And let's be clear, we're dealing with customer data, predictive models, and intellectual property. If we're not careful, we could be opening ourselves up to cybersecurity threats, regulatory violations, and technological inefficiencies."

Mehta shook his head. "AI is not just about security and compliance. It's about innovation. We need to be iterative and fast to stay ahead of the competition."

A Showdown in the Boardroom

The tension reached a peak when CEO Greaves called a meeting to address the issue. The stakes were clear: either AI remained a separate function, or it would be absorbed into IT.

Fernandes came in prepared and confident, presenting a structured plan for centralizing AI within IT. She outlined the potential cybersecurity threats, integration inefficiencies, and compliance risks of letting AI operate in an independent silo. "Our job is to safeguard ThermaDynamics," she argued. "If AI lacks proper oversight, we could be creating more problems than we solve."

To strengthen her case, she presented a risk assessment report, identifying gaps in security policies, infrastructure inconsistencies, and potential regulatory violations. "These are real threats," she emphasized. "We need a single, unified structure for AI operations."

Mehta and Navarro, however, weren't about to let their progress be derailed.

Mehta took a deep breath. "This isn't just about governance; it's about strategy. AI isn't just another tech stack. It's the foundation for our next-generation business model. We're already seeing AI driving 20% energy cost reductions in our factories. Our smart-building solutions are about to land us major contracts with sustainability-focused clients. If we want to compete, AI has to remain dynamic, customer-focused, and market-driven."

Mehta followed up. "If AI moves entirely into IT, we'll lose the speed and innovation that's given us a competitive edge. AI isn't just about infrastructure, it's about real-world impact. We need a hybrid model: IT supports AI, but AI remains directly tied to business transformation."

A Compromise, But Who Really Won?

After heated discussions, Greaves stepped in to break the deadlock. "Here's what we're going to do," he declared. "AI will not be folded entirely into IT, but we need some alignment. IT under Maria will provide governance, security, and compliance oversight, but Vikram's AI division will continue to operate with business autonomy, reporting directly to me."

Fernandes pursed her lips but nodded. She hadn't won complete control, but she had gained a role in shaping AI's implementation. Mehta caught Navarro's eye; they had secured AI's strategic independence, but they now had to ensure IT didn't slow them down.

As they left the meeting, Navarro muttered, "This isn't over."

Mehta nodded grimly. "No, but at least we're still in the fight."

Meanwhile, in another wing of the building, Fernandes was already plotting her next move. She had lost the battle, but the war was far from over. Her influence in IT meant she could impose stricter integration protocols, create bureaucratic hurdles, and slow AI's expansion through regulatory oversight.

Mehta knew it, too. He could see Fernandes' endgame clearly now. This wasn't just about governance, it was about power. And from that moment on, they were no longer colleagues locked in a debate. They were rivals in an escalating war for the future of ThermaDynamics.

Chapter 18

THE RECKONING

Every bold strategy eventually meets its moment of truth.

Make-or-Break Time

The next management team meeting was pivotal. Mehta and Navarro had reached the end of their timeline, and today was their final opportunity to prove that the twin transformation wasn't just viable, but essential for ThermaDynamics' survival. Months of internal battles, objections, and resistance had led to this moment. If they failed to present undeniable results, their journey would be over.

As the executives gathered, Greaves sat at the head of the table, his hands clasped together as he observed the room. On one side sat Richard Steele, the most vocal opponent of the twin transformation, exceptionally attending this meeting; a rare move prompted by mounting board pressure to scrutinize the initiative more closely. His usual stoic demeanor betrayed signs of impatience. Fred LaPlante had his arms crossed, while Maria Fernandes had her laptop open, ready to challenge any claims that would put AI outside of IT's jurisdiction. Across the table, Serge Closer sat quietly, unusually attentive to the discussion.

Katarina Svensson meanwhile, was flipping through a thick stack of financial reports, analyzing every number with meticulous scrutiny. Not waiting for anyone to officially start the meeting, she jumped in with a comment on the supply chain analytics team's shortfall. "We were promised $15 million in savings. We're at eight. That delta matters."

Mehta pushed back, realizing too late that he was coming across as defensive. "We've identified the bottlenecks; it's vendor onboarding. We need procurement to speed up contract approvals."

Greaves cut in sharply, "I don't want to talk about blame; let's focus on outcomes."

Mehta took a deep breath and stood up. "We've all had concerns over the past year about whether AI and sustainability initiatives are distractions or whether they provide real value to our company. Today, we are here to show you the data. Real-world results."

The Data That Changed Everything

The lights dimmed as Navarro clicked a button, projecting a series of slides onto the large screen at the front of the room. The first slide displayed key factory optimization metrics in bold green numbers:

- 20% reduction in energy costs at the Texas facility, translating into $2.2 million in annual savings.
- 28% drop in unplanned downtime, reducing maintenance expenses by $2.8 million.

Navarro gestured toward the figures. "These aren't estimates. These are the numbers from our own facility. The AI-driven systems have already been tested, iterated upon, and successfully implemented. The fears about production disruption? We mitigated them. These results were achieved without interrupting a single major production cycle."

A murmur spread across the room.

"We aren't just improving efficiency internally," Mehta continued, flipping to the next slide that detailed customer adoption of AI-powered smart solutions, "we're making sales." The slide showed the following:

- $120 million in new deals closed since rolling out smart-building solutions.
- Customer adoption rate 30% higher than originally forecasted.
- Clients using AI-powered climate control systems saw a 25% drop in energy consumption, providing tangible cost reductions.

- ICaaS pilot gaining traction, with $10 million in multi-year contracts secured, ensuring predictable recurring revenue and validating the high-margin subscription model.

Serge Closer spoke up, his voice carrying a tone of approval. "I've been watching this unfold, and I have to admit I was negative at first. But over the last two months, something changed. Our biggest clients aren't just interested in these solutions, they're actively asking for them."

He turned to Richard Steele, who had remained silent until now, his expression neutral. "Richard, let me put it this way. If we don't offer this, our competitors will. This isn't a niche trend anymore. This is the market moving toward a new standard."

In response, Steele shifted in his seat, a rare flicker of interest crossing his face. He was not one to offer praise easily, but even he could not ignore the hard numbers in front of him. Begrudgingly, he nodded. "For once, I'm seeing something I can't argue with. But I'll be watching these results closely. If this goes sideways, you'll have me to answer to."

A Watershed Moment

Fred LaPlante, ever the pragmatist, sighed and uncrossed his arms. "Operational efficiency is one thing," he admitted. "But I still worry about disruptions. If AI ever slows down production, those savings won't mean much."

Navarro held her ground. "That's why we started with controlled rollouts. We didn't force AI onto every facility at once. We tested, we iterated, and we ensured stability. We didn't disrupt production, we enhanced it."

Katarina folded her hands. "From a financial standpoint, if these results hold for another two quarters, I'll support a company-wide rollout."

Thomas Greaves looked at Richard Steele. "Richard, you said this was a war for survival. I agree. And the numbers show that AI and sustainability are not distractions, they're our competitive edge. We cannot afford to fall behind."

Steele exhaled sharply. Then, slowly, he nodded. "I won't stand in the way of progress. But," he added with a pointed look at Mehta and Navarro, "if these numbers slip, if even one of these projections doesn't hold, you both own that failure."

Mehta met his gaze. "We wouldn't have it any other way."

Greaves, recognizing the significance of the discussion, stood and publicly backed Mehta and Navarro, reinforcing their positions within the company and sending a strong message that AI-driven sustainability was now a core part of ThermaDynamics' strategy.

Then, more good news.

A day later, an important announcement circulated through the industry: the EU had officially mandated that heating and cooling systems needed to conform to strict environmental standards, starting in 2027. Navarro quickly checked the company's compliance reports and turned to Mehta with a smile. "Our products already meet these standards," she said. "This could give us a massive edge in the European market."

Chapter 19

BREAKING THE AI BARRIER

Breakthroughs happen when old industries embrace new intelligence.

Inconsistent Results

ThermaDynamics had begun to see the fruits of its twin transformation program. Factories worldwide reported measurable drops in energy consumption, supply chains ran smoother than ever, and maintenance downtime had shrunk by double-digit percentages in some regions. The transformation was taking hold, at least, where it was working.

At the monthly executive team meeting, Thomas Greaves sat at the head of the polished mahogany table, his fingers tapping an impatient rhythm against a stack of performance reports. The room hummed with cautious optimism, but Greaves' brow furrowed as he skimmed the latest numbers, his sharp eyes zeroing in on a glaring inconsistency.

"We've got factories cutting their energy use by 30%," he said, jabbing a highlighted section of the report with a hint of pride. "But some sites are barely hitting 10%. Why isn't it delivering across the board?" He wondered if they could match the $15 million annual savings he'd read about from a commodity manufacturer using smarter AI.

The question lingered, drawing Mehta's attention. He leaned forward, his expression calm but tinged with the quiet intensity of someone who'd already wrestled with the problem. He had spent weeks dissecting the data, tracing the uneven threads of success and failure across the company's global network. He had a theory and now was the moment to test it.

"We're looking at optimization the wrong way," Mehta said, his voice steady but edged with conviction.

Elena Navarro raised an eyebrow, "What do you mean?"

Mehta pulled up a comparative analysis on the conference room's wall-mounted screen, displaying side-by-side metrics from two of ThermaDynamics' top-performing facilities: one in Germany, the other in Singapore.

"We've been using AI to spot patterns, like energy spikes, waste pockets, and inefficiencies in production. The system then suggests optimizations based on those patterns." He paused, checking to ensure they followed. "But correlation isn't causation. Just because we see efficiency gains in one facility after an adjustment, like trimming HVAC runtime, doesn't mean that adjustment was the reason. We've been treating AI like a crystal ball when we should be using it to uncover what actually drives change."

Greaves leaned back, digesting Mehta's point. "You're saying the AI's been chasing surface-level trends instead of figuring out what really works?"

"Exactly," Mehta replied. "It tells us what happens when we tweak lighting or recalibrate machinery, but not why it succeeds in Hamburg and flops in Houston. We need a more sophisticated approach, one that doesn't just predict outcomes but understands the mechanisms behind them."

A Spark from the Innovation Lab

Half the world away, in a sleek, glass-walled building on ThermaDynamics' California campus, the Innovation Lab buzzed with restless energy. Launched earlier as a sandbox for bold ideas, the Lab had become a crucible for the company's wildest experiments. It was here that the first prototypes of ThermaDynamics' twin transformation strategy had emerged, a chaotic collaboration between Mehta's data scientists and AI specialists, and Navarro's team of sustainability experts, all working under the direction of Dr. Ghada Al Balushi.

Al Balushi, a wiry woman fueled by caffeine and curiosity, had spent the last few months wrestling with the same question now stumping the executive suite: why weren't the results consistent? Her team had dubbed it 'the

Consistency Conundrum,' their whiteboards a mess of equations and half-formed theories, and tables covered by coffee rings. It was Al Balushi who'd stumbled across a breakthrough during a late-night dive into academic journals: a methodology called Causal Machine Learning (Causal ML). She'd noted that companies like Netflix were already using it to optimize recommendations, proving it was more than a theory. She'd pitched it to Mehta over a frantic video call, her excitement spilling through the screen.

"Causal ML is the key," she'd told him, her voice crackling with urgency. "It's not just about spotting patterns, it's about proving what causes them. We can stop guessing and start knowing."

Mehta had been intrigued but wary. The Innovation Lab was notorious for chasing moonshots, some brilliant, others dead ends. But Al Balushi's persistence, backed by rough simulations from her team, had convinced him to bring the idea forward.

Now, standing before the executives, Mehta echoed her fervor. "For months, we've been tracking a methodology called Causal Machine Learning," he said, projecting a diagram of interconnected nodes and arrows onto the screen. "Unlike traditional machine learning, which thrives on correlation, Causal ML digs deeper. It pinpoints which actions actually drive change, cutting through the noise of coincidence. Companies like Microsoft are scaling this now; it's not just something in the lab."

LaPlante frowned, still unconvinced. "How does that help us?"

Mehta zoomed in on the German factory's data. "Right now, the AI sees that lowering temperatures correlates with reduced emissions. But it doesn't know if the temperature drop caused it, or if something else did, like a production dip. With Causal ML, we can run counterfactual simulations, virtual 'what-if' scenarios, to test whether a change delivers the effect we want. It's like seeing alternate realities without real-world risks."

A murmur rippled through the room. Greaves' eyes narrowed, but a flicker of interest sparked behind them. "So instead of guessing which AI tweaks will work, we can be sure?"

"Precisely," Mehta said. "If we build this into our system, we can track every intervention across our sites, isolate the true drivers of efficiency, and ditch changes that don't actually matter."

The Innovation Lab Steps Up

At the Innovation Lab, Ghada Al Balushi paced before her team. Mehta had texted her mid-pitch: They're listening. Get ready.

"Alright, people," Al Balushi said, clapping her hands to jolt the team from their caffeine stupor. "If this gets the go-ahead, we're not just tweaking the AI, we're reengineering it. Causal ML isn't an add-on; it's a new foundation. We need data pipelines, simulation frameworks, and a way to explain this to factory managers who'll think 'counterfactual' sounds like a bad movie plot. Plus, we'll need cleaner data than we've got to make it work across 50 factories."

One of her smartest scientists, a young physicist named Marcus Frey grinned, twirling a marker between his fingers. "I've got a prototype running already. It's rough, but it simulates three variables: temperature, production rate, and emissions for the Singapore plant. Took me all weekend."

Al Balushi stopped pacing, impressed. "Show me."

Minutes later, the team huddled around Frey' laptop as he ran the simulation. The screen displayed a graph comparing the real outcome, lowering temperatures cut emissions by 15%, against a counterfactual where temperatures held steady. The result? Emissions dropped anyway, tied to a production slowdown, not the temperature tweak.

"See?" Frey said. "The system flagged temperature as the winner, but it was a red herring. Causal ML adjusted for confounders like production rate to show the temperature tweak only had a 2% causal impact, and production drove the rest."

Al Balushi nodded, her mind racing. "And if we scale this," she said, "we could optimize supply chains or even predict customer retention, not just efficiency." If they could scale this across ThermaDynamics' 50+ facilities, they'd unlock precision no competitor could touch.

A Competitive Edge, and a Challenge

Back in the boardroom, LaPlante's disbelief began to soften. "But will this work with our messy data across 50 factories?" he asked. Mehta nodded confidently. "The Lab's been prepping for that."

"If this works," Navarro added, "it won't just fix our gaps. It'll solve one of sustainability's biggest headaches: proving our changes actually deliver value."

"More than that," Mehta continued, "every competitor's touting 'AI-driven' sustainability right now. But while they tweak blindly with AI, we'll prove our sustainability claims with hard causality. If we're the first to guarantee real, measurable impact, customers will pick us every time. It's a competitive edge we can't ignore."

Greaves exhaled, the stakes sinking in. This wasn't just about numbers, it was about ThermaDynamics' future. "How long until we can test this?"

"We've been collecting the data already," Mehta said. "The Innovation Lab's been laying the groundwork for months. If we greenlight it now, we can have pilot factories running these models within three months."

Greaves glanced around the table, reading the room. LaPlante gave a cautious nod. The CFO, quiet until now, scribbled a cost estimate but didn't push back. The momentum was undeniable.

"Alright," Greaves said, his voice resolute. "Let's build it."

The Next Frontier

As the meeting broke up, Mehta fired off a text to Al Balushi: It's a go. Three months. Her reply pinged back instantly: We're ready.

In the days that followed, the Innovation Lab sprang into action. Al Balushi's team worked around the clock, stitching together data from ThermaDynamics' factories, refining Marcus Frey's prototype, and drafting a guide to train site managers on the new approach. Mehta shuttled between the Lab and the C-suite, keeping the executives aligned as the project took shape.

Causal Machine Learning became ThermaDynamics' next frontier, a bold step beyond optimization into a realm of certainty. It wasn't just about sharpening sustainability efforts; it was about proving, beyond doubt, that they worked. For a company staking its reputation on green innovation, that proof could be the line between leading the pack and fading into the crowd. As Mehta left the boardroom, he mused that this could redefine not just sustainability, but how they ran the whole company.

Chapter 20

LEADERSHIP SHAKE-UP

*When leaders won't change,
change finds new leaders.*

The Need for a Governance Overhaul

As ThermaDynamics edged closer to fully integrating AI-driven sustainability across its products and operations, one critical challenge remained: governance. The company had survived internal battles, proved AI's viability in the market, and secured investor confidence. Yet, at the highest level, the board still operated under an outdated structure, one that had been built for an era of steady, incremental growth rather than the rapid transformation ThermaDynamics was undergoing.

The limitations of traditional governance had become increasingly apparent. The board, once effective in overseeing stable manufacturing operations, lacked the expertise and agility required for an AI-driven enterprise. Strategic decisions were slow, risk assessments outdated, and internal conflicts, such as Maria Fernandes' attempt to control AI initiatives, exposed a fractured oversight model. If ThermaDynamics was to truly lead in AI-driven sustainability, it needed a governance system that could keep pace with the complexity of emerging technologies and global regulations.

A Moment of Reckoning

During a tense quarterly board meeting, Greaves presented a sobering analysis. "We're no longer a conventional manufacturer. Our market position is now defined by AI, digital transformation, and sustainability solutions. If we don't evolve how we govern this company, we will fail, not because of competition, but because of internal inertia."

Richard Steele raised an eyebrow. "Are you saying the board isn't capable of leading this company anymore?"

"I'm saying we need to adapt," Greaves replied, carefully choosing his words. "Our expertise in operations and finance remains invaluable, but we lack strong leadership in AI, digital transformation, and sustainability. We need a governance model that reflects where we are, not where we were."

Several board members shifted in their seats, recognizing the implications. Patricia Wong, one of the newer members, nodded. "Our strategy needs to reflect the world we're operating in. This isn't just a technology shift; it's a fundamental business shift."

A New Era of Governance

In a bold move, Greaves initiated a major leadership shakeup that would reshape how the company operated.

The most significant change came with the removal of Maria Fernandes as CIO. The board had grown frustrated with IT's sluggish adoption of AI-driven initiatives, and her resistance to decentralizing AI governance had stalled progress. With Fernandes out, IT was placed under Vikram Mehta's leadership, aligning AI development and digital infrastructure under one streamlined command. This consolidation aimed to ensure seamless integration of AI-driven optimizations across all business units.

At the same time, Greaves announced changes to the board. Three long-serving members, who had built their careers in traditional manufacturing and resisted the company's AI transition, announced their retirement. They were replaced by Dr. Olivia Becker, an AI specialist; Lee Kai Shan, a former CTO of a Fortune 500 tech firm; and Dr. Sophia Martinez, a sustainability strategist with deep regulatory expertise in global environmental standards. The new board composition reflected ThermaDynamics' evolving priorities, ensuring the company's leadership had the necessary foresight to navigate an AI-driven future.

To ensure rapid decision-making, risk mitigation, and compliance alignment, Greaves also introduced an AI and Sustainability Oversight Committee. The committee, composed of AI strategists, sustainability experts, and key executives, would oversee the deployment of AI innovations, ensuring that technology and sustainability remained synchronized with the company's long-term vision.

With these structural changes, Greaves sent a clear message that ThermaDynamics was not just embracing transformation; it was restructuring itself to lead it.

Redefining Governance for an AI-Driven Future

As ThermaDynamics' twin transformation took root, Thomas Greaves saw the old governance playbook crumbling. "We're not tweaking a machine here," he'd say. "We're rewiring the whole damn system." The board couldn't just oversee anymore. It had to anticipate, adapt, and harness AI like never before.

Here's how they redefined governance to match an AI-driven, sustainable future:

- **Board composition must reflect the frontier**
  Manufacturing know-how wasn't enough anymore.
  ThermaDynamics needed minds fluent in AI and planetary stakes. Newcomers like Dr. Olivia Becker and Lee Kai Shan weren't just seat-fillers; they brought battle-tested AI chops and tech foresight. Greaves pushed for a wilder idea: what if an AI sat on the board? Not as a gimmick, but as a co-strategist crunching real-time data no human could match. The idea was tabled, for now, but the room buzzed with the possibility.

- **Decision-making goes real-time**
  Quarterly reviews felt like fossils in an AI world. The new AI & Sustainability Oversight Committee didn't just meet monthly, they tapped live dashboards tracking emissions, market shifts, and AI performance metrics. During a supply chain snag, the committee used AI predictions to pivot production in days, not weeks. "Speed's our edge," Greaves insisted, "and data's our fuel."

- **Risk management gets a broader lens**
  Finance risks were old news, AI brought ethical quagmires and regulatory minefields. When an AI model flagged a supplier for potential labor violations, the board didn't just react; they built a proactive framework. It blended AI risk scans with human judgment, catching issues before they hit headlines. Global sustainability regulations? They stayed ahead with AI simulations, not guesswork.

- **Ethics and transparency anchor AI**
  Stakeholders demanded more than profits, they wanted trust. ThermaDynamics rolled out an AI Governance Charter, promising ethical deployment and open audits. After an AI pricing tool sparked bias concerns, the board didn't dodge; they dissected it publicly, fixed it, and earned kudos from investors. "If we hide, we die," Greaves said bluntly.

- **Learning never stops**
  The board couldn't coast on past wins, AI and sustainability moved too fast. Monthly workshops with AI pioneers and green-tech leaders became mandatory. Greaves even dragged them to a global AI governance summit, where they debated regulators and rivals alike. "Ignorance isn't an option," he noted, eyeing the room.

- **ESG becomes the backbone**
  Sustainability wasn't a side hustle, it was the strategy. The board tied every big call, AI investments, supplier picks, even bonuses, to sustainability goals and social impact. When an AI-driven recycling pilot slashed waste by 20%, they didn't just celebrate; they doubled down, linking exec pay to the next milestone.

This wasn't just change, it was a revolution. Greaves knew the old guard grumbled, and some feared AI might outpace them. But he saw ThermaDynamics as not just surviving the future, but shaping it.

"We're no longer a company figuring out AI," he said. "We're a company built for it."

Transformation Takeaways: Memo to Leadership

To: Thomas Greaves, CEO

From: Elena Navarro, Chief Sustainability Officer, and Vikram Mehta, Chief AI Officer

Date: March 2027

Subject: Insights from Turning the Transformation Tide

✓ What Worked

- **Pilot success with tangible ROI.**
  The Texas factory rollout achieved measurable results: 20% energy cost reduction ($2.2M in savings), and 28% drop in unplanned downtime ($2.8M in savings), building a solid foundation of credibility.
- **Independent audit restored credibility.**
  A third-party audit confirmed the AI environmental impact, helping to counter the damaging PR from the leaked report and giving us ammunition in internal debates.
- **Workforce engagement strategy.**
  Under HR's leadership, employee adoption improved via peer-led training, contextual use cases, job security assurances, and performance incentives, humanizing AI and boosting plant-level trust.
- **Strategic Compromise on AI Governance.**
  The hybrid governance model gave IT oversight without compromising AI's business autonomy, preserving innovation speed while appeasing internal power dynamics.
- **Strong executive presentations with results.**
  Presented real data (cost savings, new revenue, reduced downtime) that directly addressed board concerns and shifted sentiment.

- **Breakthrough with causal machine learning (Causal ML).**
  The pivot to Causal ML addressed inconsistencies in performance and positioned ThermaDynamics as a leader in verifiable, impact-driven AI, moving beyond 'AI-powered' to 'AI-proven.'
- **Governance overhaul and leadership restructure.**
  Retiring board members were replaced by experts in AI and sustainability.

✘ What Didn't Work

- **Persistent internal power struggles.**
  Ongoing turf wars, especially with IT, caused unnecessary delays and morale issues, exposing cracks in alignment and organizational design.
- **PR crisis from sustainability report leak.**
  The company failed to proactively control the narrative, leading to reputational damage, investor skepticism, and lost sales momentum at a critical stage.
- **Fragmented AI implementation.**
  Early deployments lacked causal insight, leading to uneven results across factories and reinforcing board doubts about scalability.
- **Delayed customer confidence recovery.**
  Despite internal successes, external perception lagged. Sales teams struggled with client hesitancy due to reputational concerns even after internal validation.
- **Resistance from the workforce.**
  Initial rollout faced employee pushback due to fears of job loss, lack of clarity, and cultural resistance to change, costing early momentum and requiring corrective action.

📚 Lessons Learned

- **The narrative matters as much as the facts.**
  Even when results were strong, perception shaped by public trust, media, and internal politics played a massive role in determining strategic viability.

- **You must win the workforce first.**
  Empowering the people on the ground, addressing their fears, and showing real benefits in their day-to-day work is essential for any transformation.
- **Causal insight > correlation hype.**
  Without understanding what drives outcomes, AI optimization will underperform. Causal ML turned out to be a game-changing innovation for consistent, scalable impact.
- **Governance must evolve with strategy.**
  Structural inertia at the top nearly derailed progress. Real transformation required rethinking not just the technology, but the power structures guiding it.
- **Compromise can preserve momentum.**
  The hybrid AI governance model wasn't ideal for either side, but it allowed the transformation to avoid derailment by bureaucratic control.
- **Validation must be external and credible.**
  Internal proof wasn't enough, external audits, customer testimonials, and market-ready compliance were key to restoring stakeholder faith.
- **Doubters can become champions.**
  Turning skeptical figures into cautious supporters proved the power of bottom-up validation and real-world success.

Elena & Vikram

ACT 4

VICTORY AND THE ROAD AHEAD

Chapter 21

THE TRANSFORMATION OF THERMADYNAMICS

You know it worked when what once seemed radical becomes routine.

A Bold New Direction

ThermaDynamics officially pivoted towards a new business model, one that placed the twin transformation at the heart of its operations. What had once been seen as an ambitious experiment was now the company's defining strategy. The dual strategy was no longer optional, it was an existential necessity.

At a company-wide all-hands meeting, CEO Greaves took the stage, flanked by Mehta and Navarro. Employees, managers, and key stakeholders had gathered, both in person and via livestream across the company's global offices.

"This isn't just an adjustment," Greaves began, his voice carrying across the auditorium. "This is our future. ThermaDynamics is no longer just a manufacturing company. We are becoming the global leader in AI-driven sustainable building solutions."

The words landed heavily. Some employees nodded in approval, while others exchanged disbelieving glances. Greaves continued, acknowledging the concerns head-on.

"I know that change brings uncertainty, and I know that some of you are wondering if this is the right move. But let me be clear, our market is changing, and we must change with it."

He gestured toward the large screen behind him, which displayed compelling data points:
- Projected $1.5 billion market for AI-powered building efficiency solutions by 2028.
- ThermaDynamics' internal cost savings projected to reach $240 million annually by expanding AI optimization company-wide.
- Early adopters of our technology already seeing up to 30% reductions in energy consumption.
- Market capitalization trending upward to $9 billion, reflecting early successes in AI-driven sustainability initiatives.

"This is not a bet," Greaves concluded. "This is a calculated move based on data, demand, and where the world is heading."

He waved his hand and a factory shimmered into existence above the stage, its holographic guts pulsing as AI trimmed energy waste in real-time, a vision no one could ignore.

Integrating AI and Sustainability at Every Level

The company's transition wasn't just about rebranding; it required deep, structural change.
- Manufacturing operations: Factory upgrades were rolled out globally. AI-powered predictive maintenance systems reduced downtime and smart energy grids cut costs by optimizing production cycles in real time. With over 40,000 sensors installed across global manufacturing sites, energy efficiency improved dramatically.
- Product innovation: The R&D team, led by Helena Yoshida, accelerated the development of self-learning smart HVAC systems that could adapt to environmental conditions and occupancy levels. They also harnessed generative AI, letting algorithms dream up HVAC designs that slashed energy waste while cutting production time in half. These systems, integrated with real-time IoT data, provided an average $10,000 savings per commercial building annually.
- Sales and marketing overhaul: Serge Closer led an aggressive push to reposition ThermaDynamics as a solutions provider rather than just an equipment manufacturer. Sales teams were retrained to showcase

AI's ability to generate ROI for customers, not just sustainability benefits. Marketing campaigns emphasized data-backed performance improvements, highlighting real-world case studies with savings exceeding $250 million collectively.

- Employee engagement and culture shift: Saskia Schmidt introduced company-wide AI and sustainability literacy programs, ensuring employees at all levels understood and contributed to the transformation. Over 85% of employees participated in AI workshops within the first six months.

To ensure that AI sustainability objectives were embedded deeply into the company's DNA, ThermaDynamics undertook a large-scale process redesign initiative. New performance metrics were introduced across all departments, linking individual and team KPIs directly to AI and sustainability outcomes. Governance structures were revised to facilitate cross-functional collaboration, with AI sustainability objectives woven into strategic planning, procurement, and operational decision-making. By integrating these new priorities into the organization's fundamental processes, ThermaDynamics ensured that AI sustainability was not just an initiative, but an intrinsic part of how the company functioned at every level.

All new product development, for example, would include someone from IT, AI, or technology and someone from sustainability on the design team. This would ensure that every product not only met efficiency and performance goals, but also aligned with ThermaDynamics' long-term sustainability commitments. By embedding sustainability expertise directly into the design process, innovation would be balanced with environmental responsibility from the outset.

Subscription-Based Growth: The ThermaCloud™ Ecosystem

While product sales had been the primary revenue driver in the past, Greaves and his team recognized that the future lay in recurring revenue models. Instead of selling standalone AI solutions, they worked to create a scalable, subscription-based service that provided continuous value to customers.

With that in mind, Mehta spearheaded the launch of the ThermaCloud™ AI platform, a groundbreaking system born from the Innovation Lab's experimental work and accelerated by contributions from the predictive maintenance and ICaaS task forces. The platform allowed businesses to monitor, predict, and control energy use in real time and was projected to generate $300 million in annual recurring revenue within three years. ThermaCloud™ also enabled remote diagnostics, reducing onsite maintenance visits by 50%. Additionally, the ICaaS task force had worked closely to enable scalable, AI-driven climate management across client portfolios. Instead of making large capital investments in sustainable building technologies, customers could now opt for an Intelligent Cooling-as-a-Service model, paying a monthly fee to integrate ThermaDynamics' AI into their facilities. This lowered the barrier to entry and increased adoption rates dramatically.

ThermaCloud™ offered multiple tiers of service:

- Standard AI optimization: Real-time monitoring and automated energy adjustments, leading to an average energy cost reduction of 18%.
- Advanced AI efficiency suite: Predictive maintenance, automated carbon footprint reporting, and AI-powered sustainability audits, delivering energy savings of up to 35%.
- Enterprise AI partnership: Custom AI deployment tailored to corporate sustainability goals, offering deep data insights, compliance tracking, and direct integration with city-wide smart grids.
- ICaaS (Intelligent Cooling-as-a-Service): A subscription-based cooling model where AI-managed climate control ensured optimal temperature efficiency at a fixed monthly cost, eliminating upfront investment for customers while guaranteeing steady recurring revenue.

"What truly sets ThermaCloud™ apart," Mehta explained during a strategy session, "is its use of causal machine learning, allowing customers to simulate 'what-if' scenarios, like the impact of different energy strategies on their carbon footprint and costs, giving them a competitive edge over traditional solutions." This unique capability, refined from ThermaDynamics' internal AI innovations, positioned the platform as a forward-thinking tool for businesses seeking not just efficiency, but strategic insights in a sustainability-driven market.

By offering scalable solutions, ThermaDynamics ensured that businesses of all sizes could integrate AI-driven sustainability into their operations. More importantly, customer retention rates rose, as businesses saw that the cost savings far outweighed the subscription fees. Internal projections estimated that within three years, ThermaCloud™ could generate more than $300 million annually in recurring revenue, with ICaaS contributing significantly as demand for AI-powered climate management surged, solidifying its place as an industry standard.

Overcoming Resistance

Not everyone embraced the shift immediately. Not surprisingly, Richard Steele remained hesitant, warning against 'getting carried away' with new initiatives at the expense of financial stability. Fred LaPlante was reluctant to disrupt factory processes further, arguing that 'too much change, too fast' could destabilize output.

To counter these concerns, Mehta and Navarro initiated phased rollouts, ensuring that each stage of AI integration proved its value before expanding further. After successive quarters of positive results, even Steele had to acknowledge the numbers. "The market is responding," he admitted during a quarterly review. "Let's see if we can keep up."

The First Major Wins

Momentum accelerated as early adopters of ThermaDynamics' solutions reported significant cost savings. One high-profile case study came from Riverview Properties, the real estate giant that had wavered before adopting AI-driven energy management. Sarah Young and James Patel, initially skeptical, now publicly endorsed ThermaDynamics' technology after seeing a 32% reduction in building energy costs, turning them into long-term partners.

In parallel, municipal contracts were secured in New York, Berlin, and Tokyo, integrating ThermaCloud™ into smart city infrastructure. With government-backed sustainability incentives, ThermaDynamics' solutions became the preferred choice for large-scale developments, adding $500 million in projected contract revenue over five years.

Greaves, seeing the success, doubled down. "This is just the beginning," he told the board. "We've proven we can execute internally. Now, we take this further."

ThermaDynamics announced plans to expand its AI-sustainability initiatives more deeply into Europe, Asia, and the Middle East, where government incentives for green technology were at an all-time high. The company secured partnerships with municipal governments to integrate smart-building infrastructure into new city developments, positioning itself at the forefront of the smart-city revolution.

Steps in the Right Direction

By the end of the year, ThermaDynamics was no longer just a heating and cooling company. It had evolved into a full-fledged AI-driven sustainability powerhouse, setting the industry standard for integrating digital transformation into operations and products.

But the transformation was still in its early stages. Mehta and Navarro understood that early wins were just the foundation. The real test would come with scale: embedding change across global operations, ensuring consistent execution, and staying ahead in a rapidly evolving market. There were still doubters to convince, systems to upgrade, and strategies to refine.

As they exited a long leadership meeting one late afternoon, Mehta turned to Navarro and offered a half-smile. "Feels like we're finally gaining ground."

Navarro returned the smile, but her eyes remained focused. "We are. Now we just have to hold it and keep building."

Chapter 22

AI AND THE CIRCULAR ECONOMY

The smartest systems don't just optimize, they regenerate.

Expanding the Sustainability Focus

The AI-driven transformation at ThermaDynamics had already proven its worth. The projects in energy efficiency had delivered cost reductions, operational stability, and a clear path toward full-scale rollout. But for Navarro, something was still missing.

"We're optimizing energy," she said one evening in the war room, studying factory reports. "But what about the materials? How much are we still wasting?"

Mehta looked up from his screen, intrigued. "How much do you think?"

Navarro tapped the report in front of her. "More than we should. Scrap materials, overproduced parts, discarded components that could be repurposed, it's millions of dollars being thrown away. We're running an AI-powered factory, but our waste streams are still operating like it's the 1990s."

Mehta sat back, considering. AI had already optimized energy consumption, predictive maintenance, and production scheduling, but raw material efficiency hadn't been touched. "You're thinking circular economy?"

"Exactly," Navarro nodded. "AI is making our factories smarter, but what if it could make our entire supply chain self-sustaining? Instead of discarding materials, we could reuse, repurpose, and optimize. AI isn't just about efficiency, it's about intelligence. And right now, our waste management is horrible."

The Circular Economy Challenge

Despite the advances in AI-driven manufacturing, ThermaDynamics still had a major waste problem.

- Overproduction: Forecasting errors led to excess components and raw materials piling up, increasing storage and disposal costs.
- Defective components: Malfunctioning or slightly flawed parts were being discarded rather than salvaged or repurposed.
- Inefficient recycling: The company had no system in place to track and reintegrate leftover materials back into production.
- No product take-back program: The company lacked any mechanism to reclaim and recycle old products from customers at end-of-life. This created a significant missed opportunity to recover valuable materials and components.

At the next leadership meeting, Navarro laid out the case. "We can't claim to be a sustainability leader if our factories and our customers are dumping tons of materials every month. AI needs to optimize not just our energy consumption, but our entire resource flow."

CFO Svensson, ever the pragmatist, folded her arms. "And how much is this going to cost us?"

Navarro didn't miss a beat. "It's not a cost. It's a recovery. We're spending millions on new raw materials while throwing away usable scraps. AI can track materials, assess quality, and redirect resources to where they're needed most. We could cut waste by at least 30% in the first year."

Svensson raised an eyebrow, "That sounds optimistic."

Mehta jumped in. "We don't have to guess. We can simulate it before making any major changes."

That was when the team decided to integrate AI-powered circular economy models into their digital twin simulation, testing how AI could reconfigure waste, overproduction, and resource allocation before rolling it out in the real world.

The Smart Materials Network

Using machine learning and real-time sensor tracking, ThermaDynamics launched an AI-driven material tracking system capable of:

- Predicting overproduction: AI analyzed historical sales, factory output, and market demand to adjust manufacturing volumes dynamically, reducing excess inventory by 25% in early tests.
- Reintroducing defective components: Instead of scrapping faulty parts, AI categorized them as repairable, reusable, or recyclable, enabling 40% of previously discarded materials to be reintegrated.
- Automating sustainable procurement: The system scanned supplier data to source materials from recycled or sustainable sources, reducing reliance on virgin raw materials by 18%.
- Designing for circularity: The AI platform now evaluated new product designs for disassembly potential, material recoverability, and component reuse. Early prototypes showed that products designed with this system could achieve 85% material recovery at end-of-life, compared to just 12% with conventional designs, while reducing manufacturing costs by 7% through standardized components.

The Challenges of Implementation

Despite the promising results, implementing AI-driven circular economy solutions posed several challenges.

Navarro was on a visit to a supplier facility in her native Spain. The factory hummed with promise, but beneath the surface, chaos loomed. She was standing with the supplier's head of production, a grizzled holdout from the old guard. He was shaking his head, and Navarro could anticipate what he was about to say.

"You want us to rework our entire production line for your circular strategy? That's a logistical nightmare. We'll have to charge you a lot more. If you really want it, it's going to cost you."

Legacy suppliers like this one, stuck in a pre-digital dark age, bristled at tracking every scrap, their resistance a stubborn wall Navarro couldn't yet crack. Meanwhile, Mehta wrestled with a different beast: data. The AI churned through a flood of real-time numbers, straining sensors and processors to the brink as it sorted reusable steel from recyclable plastic. Upgrades weren't optional; they were a lifeline, and the clock was ticking.

Across the room, workers grumbled as they fumbled with new material classification tasks, their hands hesitant, eyes wary.

"More work, less control," one muttered, echoing a fear of automation that hung heavy in the air.

Navarro knew retraining wasn't enough, they needed a full-on culture shift to win them over. Then there were the regulators, every region a maze of shifting rules, from California's strict waste laws to Europe's patchwork demands. The AI had to bend, twist, and adapt without missing a beat, a highwire act that kept Mehta up nights tweaking algorithms. And the kicker? Retrofitting the production lines with waste-tracking tech wasn't cheap. It required millions upfront, a gamble that had CFO Svensson breathing down their necks, demanding proof the savings would outweigh the cost.

This wasn't a smooth rollout; it was a fight on five fronts, suppliers digging in, data threatening to drown them, workers pushing back, rules shifting beneath their feet, and the budget teetering on a razor's edge. Yet as Navarro and Mehta locked eyes across the buzzing factory, a shared resolve sparked between them. Already, whispers of victory were seeping through the chaos, manufacturing scrap down 17%, supply chain delays cut by 18%, and $5 million clawed back from defective parts. If they could break through these barriers, those numbers wouldn't just be a fleeting win, they'd be the opening salvo in a revolution poised to reshape the industry.

Building a Circular Ecosystem

What started as an internal transformation at ThermaDynamics soon revealed broader potential. Navarro and Mehta realized that the company's AI-driven circular economy model wasn't limited to its own operations—it could extend into a wider ecosystem. They saw an opportunity not just to improve their supply chain, but to build a collaborative network of partners that could collectively advance industrial sustainability.

"We're not an island," Navarro said during a strategy session, her tone resolute. "If we want true circularity, we need to bring everyone along, suppliers, customers, even other industries. AI gives us the tools to connect them all."

The vision was ambitious: create a circular ecosystem, a coalition of partners committed to leveraging ThermaDynamics' AI technology to eliminate waste and maximize resource efficiency across multiple sectors. The ecosystem would include:

- Suppliers: Incentivized to adopt AI-driven tracking systems for raw materials, ensuring that every component entering ThermaDynamics' production lines came from sustainable or recycled sources. Early pilots with key suppliers showed a 20% reduction in virgin material use.
- Customers: Encouraged to integrate ThermaDynamics' smart materials network into their own operations, sharing data on product usage and end-of-life disposal to close the loop. Titan Motors, for instance, agreed to a data-sharing partnership that allowed ThermaDynamics to refine its AI models for automotive-specific waste streams.
- Technology providers: Companies specializing in IoT sensors, blockchain for supply chain transparency, and advanced recycling tech were brought on board to enhance the ecosystem's capabilities. A partnership with a blockchain firm enabled real-time tracking of materials from production to recycling, boosting transparency by 35%.
- Industry peers: In a bold move, ThermaDynamics invited select competitors, like CoolTech Industries, to join pilot programs, sharing anonymized AI insights to elevate industry-wide standards. While hesitant, CoolTech agreed to a limited trial, recognizing the mutual benefit of reducing sector-wide waste.

Building this ecosystem wasn't without hurdles. Suppliers balked at initial integration costs, and some customers worried about data privacy. Mehta addressed these concerns by rolling out a phased onboarding process, starting with a core group of 10 partners and proving the model's value with hard data, $15 million in collective savings within the first six months.

The ecosystem quickly gained traction. By connecting disparate players through AI-driven analytics, ThermaDynamics created a self-reinforcing network where every participant benefited: suppliers cut costs, customers reduced their environmental footprint, and the company solidified its leadership in circular innovation.

"This isn't just about us anymore," Mehta told the leadership team. "It's about building an industry standard where circularity is the norm."

Steele's Reluctant Approval

At the next board meeting, Steele sat quietly as the data poured in. Circular economy AI had generated $50 million in cost savings, secured new clients, and positioned ThermaDynamics as the undisputed leader in sustainable manufacturing.

Then he spoke. "Fine. I'll admit it. This AI waste-reduction thing… it works."

Greaves smiled. "We prefer to call it circular intelligence."

Even Steele chuckled at that.

Scaling the Circular Economy Model

With AI-driven material optimization proving successful, ThermaDynamics prepared to scale the model to all of its global operations. The next step? Full automation of circular supply chains using real-time AI analytics.

On the way to a supplier meeting, Mehta turned to Navarro. "We started with AI-driven energy management. Now we're optimizing entire industries."

Navarro grinned. "And we're still just getting started."

Chapter 23

CUSTOMER BEHAVIOR

*Change the habits, not the values,
and loyalty follows.*

The Unfinished Puzzle

ThermaDynamics had revolutionized its operations. AI-driven systems had optimized energy use, predictive maintenance had slashed downtime, and circular economy principles had drastically reduced waste. Yet, as Mehta and Navarro looked at the broader picture, something wasn't adding up.

"We've done everything we can inside our walls," Navarro said, flipping through the latest sustainability reports. "We've cut emissions, improved efficiency, and built net-zero factories. But if we stop here, we're only solving half the problem."

Mehta frowned. "You're talking about what happens after our products leave the factory."

"Exactly." She turned her screen toward him. "Even with all our sustainability efforts, a product's full environmental footprint depends just as much on how it's used as how it's made. And we have no control over that."

Mehta reflected for a moment. "We need to influence customer behavior."

The realization was daunting. Unlike their controlled manufacturing environments, customer behavior was unpredictable. Companies could design the most energy-efficient systems in the world, but if clients ignored efficiency settings, delayed maintenance, or mismanaged resources, all the gains were erased.

And that's exactly what was happening.

The Sustainability Gap: Technology vs. Behavior

ThermaDynamics had seen it firsthand. After installing AI-powered energy management in commercial properties, early data showed a 25% drop in energy use. But within months, efficiency started slipping.

Building managers were manually overriding AI recommendations. Facility teams reverted to old habits. Employees left inefficient systems running, thinking the difference was negligible.

Navarro rubbed her forehead in frustration. "We designed these systems to optimize efficiency automatically. Why are people fighting against them?"

Mehta leaned back in his chair. "Because people don't trust what they don't understand. And if you give them an override button, they'll use it. We can make the smartest systems in the world, but if customers don't use them correctly, none of it matters."

It was a sobering truth. Sustainability wasn't just a technology problem. It was a human behavior problem.

The Psychology of Change: Why Customers Resist Sustainability

ThermaDynamics wasn't alone in this challenge. Across industries, companies struggled to get customers to use products in the most sustainable way.

The most significant barrier to adoption wasn't technological but human. People consistently prioritized convenience over efficiency, preferring familiar manual settings to AI-driven recommendations, even when this choice increased their long-term costs. The comfort of the known outweighed the promised benefits of the unknown, regardless of the data supporting those benefits.

Unlike visible forms of waste, energy inefficiency remained largely hidden—building managers wouldn't see the consequences of overriding an AI temperature optimization until the utility bill arrived weeks later, and even then, they often failed to make the connection. This disconnect between action and consequence made it difficult for users to recognize the value of AI-driven efficiency measures in real-time.

The problem was compounded by a deep-seated mistrust of automation, with customers viewing AI-driven decisions as mysterious 'black boxes' that threatened their sense of control. Many facility managers who had spent decades fine-tuning systems manually were reluctant to cede that responsibility to an algorithm they couldn't see or fully understand, regardless of its proven effectiveness.

Perhaps most challenging was the phenomenon of change fatigue, where sustainability initiatives were perceived as additional burdens rather than labor-saving innovations. Though AI systems were specifically designed to reduce human effort, perception trumped reality—when sustainability felt complicated, resistance naturally followed. Users already overwhelmed by technological change were quick to dismiss new systems as just another complication in their already complex work environments.

"So what do we do?" Navarro asked. "We can't force customers to use our systems correctly."

"No," replied Mehta, "but we can nudge them in the right direction."

Embedding Sustainability in Customer Behavior

Navarro, Mehta, LaPlante, and Closer met in the war room to discuss the situation with Titan Motors, a major client. The air was thick with frustration as Navarro paced before a wall of screens flickering with the latest data. "We've built the smartest systems in the world," she snapped, jabbing a finger at the override stats, "and they're still undoing it all. Why?"

Fred LaPlante shrugged, his voice curt. "Because they don't trust it, Elena. Give them a button to push, and they'll push it, damn the savings."

Mehta, hunched over his tablet, looked up sharply. "Then we take the button away, or we make it so they don't want to touch it." He tapped the screen, pulling up ThermaCloud™'s interface. "What if we lock efficiency as the default? Adjustments happen silently, lights dim, cooling shifts, unless they actively choose otherwise. Make sustainability the path of least resistance."

Navarro stopped pacing, her eyes narrowing. "Invisible sustainability," she murmured, a spark igniting. "No effort, no choice, just results."

Serge Closer grinned from the corner, ever the pragmatist. "I like it, but they need to see the payoff. Show them dollars bleeding out every time they override, right there on the dashboard, live. Titan's managers won't ignore a red number screaming $500 wasted."

"And let's make it fun," Mehta added, his voice picking up speed. "Turn it into a game, pit their factories against each other, rank them against the industry. They'll chase efficiency just to win."

Navarro nodded, her mind racing. "And reward them for it, discounts, badges, something tangible. Make green the easy choice and the smart one."

By the time the meeting ended, the screens glowed with a new vision, not a mandate, but a seduction, luring customers into sustainability one effortless, rewarding step at a time.

The new plan focused on influencing behavior without forcing change. Instead of demanding customers adapt, ThermaDynamics would make sustainable choices feel effortless, beneficial, and even rewarding.

Case Study: Titan Motors' Behavioral Shift

Mark Hensley, Titan Motors' seasoned facilities manager, squinted at the new ThermaCloud™ dashboard glowing on his desk. He'd spent years tweaking the factory's systems by gut instinct. But today felt different. The settings were locked, lights dimmed on their own, the hum of the HVAC softened without his say-so. "Effortless Sustainability," they'd called it, and damn if it didn't feel like it.

Then the screen flared to life, a sharp red alert: 'Override Cost: $320.' He looked down from his window at the factory floor. He could see that someone had overridden the AI's recommendation to reduce power to the annealing furnaces during the midday energy peak. He rushed down to investigate.

"These machines need consistent heat," insisted one of the operators. "I've been running them for twenty years." It was the third override this week, each one erasing hours of efficiency gains. "Those overrides cost us $4,700 last month," Hensley said, pointing to the highlighted figure. "The AI wasn't reducing power randomly, it was responding to grid demand signals that would have saved us peak pricing." Reluctantly, the operator allowed Hensley to reverse his override, watching dubiously as the system rebalanced.

Later, at the shift meeting, the crew crowded around an augmented reality overlay beaming from the dashboard, projecting savings right onto the humming machinery. "Look at that," one technician whistled. "We're beating the Chicago plant by 5% this week!" A leaderboard blinked 'Facility Rankings' and Hensley felt a twinge of pride. Sustainability was no longer just a chore; it was a race they could win.

By month's end, his inbox pinged with a ThermaDynamics badge, Silver Sustainability Tier, and a note about a discount on their next service contract. Mark chuckled. Green wasn't so bad when it paid off like this. The transformation was addictive. Within weeks, the factory buzzed with a new rhythm, less resistance, more collaboration. Manual overrides plummeted by a jaw-dropping 68%, as workers traded stubbornness for savings they could see and feel. Energy efficiency soared, spiking 31% as AI took the reins, fine-tuning every hum and whir of Titan's machinery. Six months in, the numbers told a story of triumph: Titan slashed $18 million off its annual operational costs, a fortune reclaimed from waste and inefficiency.

This wasn't just a win for ThermaDynamics, it was a revolution in the making. Titan Motors, once a symbol of industrial might, became a beacon of sustainable innovation, proving that even the toughest skeptics could be won over when technology met human ingenuity head-on. For Navarro and Mehta, it was more than a case study; it was the moment they knew their vision could conquer not just factories, but the hearts and minds of those who ran them.

The Shift from Selling Products to Selling Behavior

At the next management team meeting, Navarro presented the results.

"Sustainability isn't just about technology anymore," she said. "It's about how people use that technology."

Greaves smiled. "So now, we're not just in AI. We're in psychology, incentives, and customer engagement?"

Navarro shrugged. "If that's what it takes to make sustainability stick, yes."

Chapter 24

SCALING FOR THE FUTURE

True scale isn't about repetition,
it's about rhythm, reach, and resilience.

The Road to Global Expansion

With ThermaDynamics successfully pivoting to an AI-driven sustainable building solutions provider, the challenge now shifted from proving feasibility to scaling at speed. The leadership team, led by Greaves, Mehta, Navarro, LaPlante, Closer, and Schmidt, faced a monumental task, transforming an already massive operation into a fully digital, global powerhouse without losing momentum. This was not just about growth; it was about ensuring long-term dominance in an industry undergoing rapid disruption.

At a senior strategy session, Greaves stood before a conference room packed with executives, product managers, and analysts. The walls were lined with projections, market trends, and aggressive revenue targets. The air was thick with anticipation as he cleared his throat and began.

"We've validated our model. We've proven that twin transformation isn't just viable, it's necessary. Now, we execute at scale. The global demand for AI-driven sustainability is growing exponentially, and we are in the perfect position to lead this transformation. But our competitors won't wait for us. If we don't seize this moment, someone else will."

The team had identified four core areas that would drive the next stage of ThermaDynamics' expansion:
1. Expanding AI-driven sustainability solutions internationally.
2. Building long-term customer relationships through subscription-based services.
3. Optimizing internal operations to support rapid global growth without inefficiencies.
4. Reducing carbon footprint through sustainable practices and energy-efficient initiatives.

Each of these pillars presented its own opportunities and challenges, requiring a carefully crafted strategy to ensure smooth execution.

Rapid International Growth through Strategic Partnerships and Subscription-Based Services

ThermaDynamics had already secured municipal contracts in New York, Berlin, and Tokyo, but the true opportunity lay in emerging markets, where energy efficiency mandates and sustainability incentives were driving an urgent shift toward AI-powered infrastructure solutions. International expansion had to be swift yet deliberate, ensuring that AI-driven solutions were tailored to meet the distinct energy needs of different regions.

Asia-Pacific was a natural first target. The company had established a regional headquarters in Singapore, positioning itself as a gateway into China, India, Japan, Indonesia, and Australia, all markets aggressively investing in smart infrastructure. Initial market research projected a staggering $750 million in potential revenue within five years, but entering these markets required more than just launching products. It meant navigating complex regulatory landscapes, building strong partnerships with local governments, and customizing AI algorithms to adapt to vastly different energy consumption patterns and climates. ThermaDynamics introduced subscription-based models in the region, fostering long-term customer relationships by offering ongoing optimization and adaptive maintenance services tailored specifically to local conditions.

In Europe, ThermaDynamics took a different approach. With EU carbon reduction laws tightening, the company focused on developing AI-powered solutions tailored for aging infrastructures. The R&D division, led by Helena Yoshida, engineered localized heat recovery and energy optimization systems designed specifically for Europe's historic buildings, many of which had previously been resistant to modern energy upgrades. By coupling these solutions with subscription-based service packages, ThermaDynamics secured long-term partnerships with municipalities and businesses, ensuring continuous efficiency improvements and compliance with evolving sustainability standards. The results were groundbreaking: some cities saw emission reductions of up to 40% while simultaneously cutting operational costs. With these early successes, expansion into Paris, London, and Amsterdam became inevitable.

In North America, the company pivoted its focus toward commercial real estate and industrial clients. Major U.S. real estate firms, including Fortune 500 companies, saw ThermaDynamics' AI-driven climate control systems as a solution to growing regulatory pressure and rising energy costs. What began as a few key contracts quickly snowballed into a major strategic shift for the industry. Instead of simply selling smart-building systems, ThermaDynamics now offered subscription-based services designed to build and maintain long-term customer relationships, positioning itself as an indispensable partner in corporate sustainability planning.

Internal Scaling: Strengthening the Operational Backbone

Rapid expansion required a fundamental overhaul of ThermaDynamics' internal operations. AI-driven sustainability solutions were in high demand, but could the company scale quickly enough to keep up?

Manufacturing was the first priority. New AI-optimized smart factories were opened in Germany and Texas, where AI-driven robotics and real-time supply chain monitoring allowed for a 22% reduction in production time and a 19% decrease in material waste. By leveraging AI to predict demand and optimize procurement logistics, the company could ramp up production without unnecessary cost increases.

HR leader Saskia Schmidt took charge of workforce transformation. AI was an enabler, not a replacement, and she ensured that employees saw the shift as an opportunity rather than a threat. Within two years, 85% of

ThermaDynamics' workforce had undergone AI upskilling programs, ensuring they could seamlessly integrate with the company's rapidly evolving technology landscape.

Meanwhile, IT infrastructure had to scale alongside operations. The expansion allowed the company to roll out new AI updates instantaneously, creating a self-improving system that adapted to evolving customer needs.

Carbon Footprint Reduction: Minimization Before Offsets

ThermaDynamics prioritized deep emission reductions first, using AI-powered optimization, material circularity, and sustainable supply chain practices before considering any offsetting measures for residual emissions.

- Scope 1 and 2 emissions dropped by 40%, driven primarily by AI-managed renewable energy, energy efficiency, and electrification of key operations.
- Scope 3 emissions, which accounted for 87% of the company's total carbon footprint, were addressed through supplier reforms. AI-powered supplier tracking helped cut Scope 3 emissions by 25% in three years.
- Total carbon emissions decreased from 2,450 kilotons CO_2eq in 2025 to 1,780 kilotons CO_2eq in 2027.

Mehta pointed to the AI projections for Scope 3 emissions cuts. "We'll use a human-in-the-loop approach to ensure our models don't miss critical factors, embedding ethical AI principles to prioritize transparency and accountability," he said. "Our experts will review every recommendation, aligning AI with our science-based goals."

ThermaDynamics committed to ensuring that 70% of its global manufacturing footprint achieved net-zero emissions by 2032. The final 10% of residual emissions, primarily from supply chain limitations, would be offset only after every feasible direct reduction had been implemented.

The company also unveiled its AI-optimized industrial sites:

- AI-managed solar arrays and wind integration meant that 90% of the site's energy was sourced on-site, reducing grid reliance.
- Smart thermal storage allowed the facility to store excess energy, making it net-positive for eight months of the year.

Breaking Down the Walls: Embracing Open Innovation

For too long, ThermaDynamics had leaned heavily on its internal R&D teams to drive both AI and sustainability initiatives. While this insular approach had produced credible successes like ThermaCloud™, the world outside was racing forward advancing in AI, in materials science, and in clean energy technologies. Despite some early attempts to embrace open innovation initiatives, progress remained slow and fragmented. ThermaDynamics was still largely operating within its own four walls, cautious and protective of its legacy strengths.

By early 2028, Navarro and Mehta had reached a quiet but urgent conclusion: internal ingenuity alone would not be enough. They recognized that the company's hesitation to fully partner with startups, researchers, and disruptive external players had already delayed critical breakthroughs in next-generation energy storage and carbon-negative materials. To accelerate and scale the twin transformation, they needed to tear down the barriers, cultivating a new era of open innovation where outside ideas, expertise, and technologies could flow into ThermaDynamics as freely as ideas once flowed out.

The Sustainability Impact Fund & Global Engagement

ThermaDynamics created the Sustainability Impact Fund not as an exercise in corporate philanthropy but as a strategic investment designed to generate long-term value for both shareholders and the planet. CFO Katarina Svensson spearheaded this initiative, emphasizing that genuine sustainability required collaboration across borders, and suggesting a strategic approach to global engagement by partnering with innovators, governments, and research institutions worldwide. Under the CFO's leadership, the fund served as a catalyst for international cooperation, strategically investing in technologies and initiatives addressing global environmental challenges while simultaneously aligning with the company's growth strategy. Through this global engagement, ThermaDynamics sought not only financial returns but also lasting positive impacts on communities, ecosystems, and industries around the world.

- $250 million was allocated to AI-driven sustainability startups, focusing on energy storage, smart water management, and carbon-negative materials.
- By 2030, the fund aimed to back over 100 sustainability-focused AI companies worldwide, creating a pipeline of innovation that could integrate directly into ThermaDynamics' supply chain.
- Rather than simply donating to environmental causes, the fund prioritized AI-driven efficiency solutions that reduced waste, optimized resources, and opened new revenue streams, ensuring that sustainability and profitability advanced in tandem.

Instead of donating to environmental causes, where $1 spent would generate the same impact as $1 spent by anyone else, the fund focused on AI-driven sustainability innovations that lowered costs, reduced risk exposure, and opened new revenue streams, directly benefiting stakeholders. At the same time, these investments would deliver real, scalable social impact by reducing waste, optimizing resource use, improving industrial efficiency, and supporting job creation and skill development in underserved regions.

At a leadership roundtable, a board member raised concerns: "Wouldn't it be easier to just donate a percentage of revenue to green initiatives?"

Navarro responded with conviction. "That's not how real change happens. If we want sustainability to be more than a side project, we need to embed it into our business strategy. The best way for businesses to contribute to society isn't through charity, it's by leveraging innovation to drive economic and environmental progress simultaneously."

The Leadership Imperative: Unifying the Company

While external expansion was moving quickly, ThermaDynamics still needed internal alignment. The leadership team convened in a high-stakes summit, recognizing that a fragmented organization could be just as dangerous as external competition.

"We've captured market attention," Mehta said, scanning the room. "But that's not enough. We need total operational unity to ensure ThermaDynamics isn't just another player in AI-driven sustainability, we want to be the definitive leader."

Greaves nodded. "We don't just sell technology, we sell transformation. Every employee, every partner, every customer must believe in what we are doing."

Navarro shifted in her seat. "That means no more internal silos. Sales, IT, manufacturing, R&D, everyone needs to be fully aligned. We've proven that AI works. Now, we need to deliver at scale."

By the end of the summit, a new strategy was in place. ThermaDynamics would not just expand, it would redefine how businesses approached AI and sustainability. The company was not just selling products. It was selling the future.

Chapter 25

A MARKET RESURGENCE

The market doesn't reward transformation,
it rewards performance shaped by it.

The Investor Summit

With ThermaDynamics' transformation nearly complete, Wall Street had taken notice. The company's stock had recovered from its lowest points, but analysts were divided. Some saw ThermaDynamics as a leader in AI-driven sustainability, while others viewed it as an over-leveraged experiment that could collapse under competitive pressure.

The annual Investor Summit was the final proving ground. Mehta, Navarro, and CEO Thomas Greaves knew that convincing institutional investors of the company's long-term viability was as critical as winning customers. Without continued financial backing, expansion plans would stall, and competitors would gain ground.

As Greaves stepped onto the stage, Navarro and Mehta following behind him, the room filled with murmurs of anticipation. A slide was shown, displaying key financial indicators: revenue growth, market share expansion, and AI adoption rates.

"Good afternoon. Three years ago, ThermaDynamics was at a crossroads. Today, we stand as the industry leader in AI-driven sustainability," Greaves began, his voice steady. "We made bold decisions, and now, the results speak for themselves."

The next slide revealed stark numbers:

- Revenue Growth: Up 18% YoY, the highest in a decade.
- Cost Savings: Over $200 million annually from AI-driven optimizations.
- AI Market Share: 35% of the AI-driven building automation market, a doubling in just 24 months.
- New Contracts: Over $150 million in AI-powered infrastructure deals secured in the past two quarters.

A new slide followed, highlighting key performance metrics:

Year	Revenue Growth	Market Capitalization	Emissions (kilotons CO_2eq)
2025	Down 8%	$8 billion	2,450
2026	Flat	$7.5 billion	2,200
2027	Up 10%	$9 billion	1,780
2028	Up 18%	$10.56 billion	Further reduced

An analyst broke the silence from the front row. "Those are strong numbers, but growth alone doesn't guarantee long-term stability. What happens when competitors catch up? How do you ensure ThermaDynamics isn't just riding a temporary AI hype wave?"

Navarro, anticipating this question, took the floor. "Sustainability isn't a trend. It's the future of corporate responsibility and cost efficiency. Regulations are tightening worldwide. By 2030, every major commercial property in the EU and North America will be required to meet carbon reduction mandates. Our solutions make that compliance effortless. This isn't hype, it's necessity."

A skeptical investor raised his hand. "And what about margins? AI-driven solutions are expensive to maintain. Will this pivot sustain profitability?"

Mehta responded, "That's why we built ThermaCloud™ as a recurring revenue model. With over 80% of our AI customers on multi-year contracts, we've secured $300 million in annual recurring revenue, making us financially stable beyond one-off product sales. AI doesn't just sell, it retains customers."

The final test came from an institutional investor representing a multi-billion-dollar fund. "Convince me why I should double my firm's investment in ThermaDynamics. What's next?"

Greaves took a deep breath. "We're not just selling AI. We're redefining how industries operate. The next phase? Net-zero factories, AI-driven supply chains, and energy-positive buildings. We're not adapting to the future, we're creating it."

The room fell silent, then applause erupted. The investor nodded. "You've got our support."

By the end of the summit, ThermaDynamics' stock had jumped 15% in a single day, solidifying its position as the leader in AI-driven sustainability.

As Mehta and Navarro stepped off the stage, he exhaled. "I think we just won the game."

Navarro shook her head with a smile.

The Stock Rebound

The next day, ThermaDynamics' stock price continued to surge, smashing its five-year high, and a wave of vindication swept through the company's leadership team. After years of internal battles, public misgivings, and corporate infighting, the company had emerged stronger than ever. Investors who had once doubted the company's direction were now scrambling to increase their holdings, and analysts who had criticized the twin transformation push were rewriting their forecasts.

Institutional investors had taken notice of the company's impressive 18% reduction in operating costs, driven largely by AI-powered efficiency measures. Several major investment firms, including Goldman & Reed and Pacific Trust, publicly upgraded ThermaDynamics' rating to a 'strong buy,' forecasting continued revenue growth for at least the next five years.

For years, competitors like CoolTech Industries and GreenWave Solutions had dominated the energy-efficient manufacturing space. But as AI-powered energy management took center stage, ThermaDynamics began to eclipse its rivals. GreenWave, once considered an industry leader, saw its stock price stagnate at $64 per share, unable to match the AI-driven cost savings that ThermaDynamics was offering. Meanwhile, CoolTech reported a 7% decline in quarterly revenue, attributing the loss to clients shifting toward smarter, automated solutions, solutions only ThermaDynamics was providing at scale.

Outpacing the Competition

For the first time in its history, ThermaDynamics had surpassed CoolTech Industries, its largest competitor, in annual revenue growth. AI-enabled energy optimization systems had become a gold standard in the industry, and major commercial clients, from global real estate developers to industrial manufacturers, were signing multi-year contracts for ThermaDynamics' smart-building solutions.

The shift was seismic. CoolTech's CEO, Mark Drexler, admitted in an interview that his company had underestimated AI's role in industrial sustainability. "We thought smart technology would complement energy efficiency, we didn't realize it was the efficiency," he stated. Meanwhile, GreenWave announced an emergency restructuring, cutting 15% of its workforce as it struggled to compete in the AI-driven market.

Serge Closer, Head of Sales, had become one of the biggest champions of the AI strategy. "We used to struggle to differentiate ourselves from the competition," he admitted in a meeting with the board. "Now? We're setting the pace. Clients aren't just looking for efficiency anymore; they want resilience, adaptability, and sustainability, and we're the only ones delivering all three at scale."

Reflection and Resolve

That evening, Mehta and Navarro sat on the balcony of the ThermaDynamics headquarters, watching the distant London skyline as it pulsed with energy. It was a moment of quiet celebration, a rare pause in the relentless pace of transformation.

"We almost didn't make it," Mehta admitted, swirling the ice in his glass. "There were times I thought this would all fall apart."

Navarro leaned on the railing, her gaze fixed on the distant neon-lit billboards, one of which now prominently displayed an ad for ThermaDynamics' latest smart-energy solution. "We came close to failing more than once," she agreed.

Chapter 26

THE FUTURE IS HERE

The future isn't predicted.
It's built, day by difficult day.

A New Era for Manufacturing

The ribbon-cutting ceremony at ThermaDynamics' first fully AI-optimized, net-zero emissions factory was not just a corporate milestone, it was a defining moment in the company's history.

It was July 2028, and a crowd of executives, engineers, factory workers, clients, and media personnel gathered at the state-of-the-art facility, located on the outskirts of Chicago. The building itself was a monument to innovation, powered entirely by renewable energy sources and optimized by a vast network of AI-driven systems. Smart grids adjusted power consumption in real-time, while self-learning algorithms continuously monitored and improved production efficiency. Every piece of equipment, from assembly lines to robotic maintenance units, operated in synchronization with AI-driven energy management systems, ensuring that no watt was wasted and no process was redundant.

For Vikram Mehta and Elena Navarro, this was the culmination of years of struggle, resistance, and relentless determination. They had fought for this moment, against doubters, financial constraints, and internal pushback, and now, the results stood before them in steel, glass, and precision automation.

The Skeptic's Approval

At the entrance of the Chicago facility stood Richard Steele, his sharp eyes scanning the AI-powered operations humming within. Even now, after all the evidence and success, Steele remained cautious. But he wasn't blind to results. He watched as an assembly line, once prone to frequent slowdowns, now ran with flawless precision, guided by AI-driven predictive maintenance. Overhead, solar panels adjusted autonomously, tilting at the perfect angle to maximize energy absorption. Nearby, a digital dashboard displayed real-time efficiency metrics, showing a 42% reduction in overall energy consumption compared to previous-generation factories.

Steele turned to Mehta, who stood beside him, watching the factory floor with quiet satisfaction. "I wasn't convinced about this at all," Steele muttered, his voice edged with reluctant admiration. "But you proved me wrong."

Mehta extended a hand. After a brief hesitation, Steele shook it. A symbolic gesture, one that marked the turning point from resistance to acceptance.

As they walked through the facility, workers gathered around new AI-optimized terminals, adjusting to the technology that once made them uneasy. The autonomous systems didn't replace them; instead, they enhanced their capabilities. AI-driven robots handled the most physically demanding and repetitive tasks, freeing workers to focus on higher-skilled roles like systems analysis and maintenance.

One technician, a veteran of the industry, ran his hand along a new AI-assisted quality control scanner. "I never thought I'd say this," he admitted, "but these systems actually make our jobs better. No more guessing when something's about to fail. We fix things before they break."

Another engineer, overseeing the robotic assembly line, smiled as the AI-guided arms adjusted in real time to compensate for slight variances in material input. "This is what efficiency looks like," he mused. "No waste, no downtime. Just precision."

A few feet away, Sarah Young, the facilities manager from Riverview Properties, observed the factory's smart-grid system in action. "This is exactly what we've been looking for," she said, turning to Navarro. "The sustainability improvements here align perfectly with our corporate goals. If all your facilities operate at this level, you're going to lead this industry."

Navarro smiled. "That's the plan."

In the background, investors and analysts whispered among themselves, taking in the seamless integration of AI and sustainability. The numbers spoke for themselves: 30% faster production cycles, and - thanks to the advanced systems implemented at the Chicago factory - 40% lower emissions and 40% less energy consumption compared to legacy systems. Competitors would struggle to keep up.

Looking Ahead

As the event approached its end, reporters gathered around Mehta and Navarro for comments, flashing cameras and recording every word. This factory wasn't just a win for ThermaDynamics, it was a case study in what was possible when AI and sustainability worked together.

"What's next for ThermaDynamics?" one journalist asked.

Mehta exchanged a look with Navarro before answering. "We scale further," he said with conviction. "This factory is just the beginning. We're already planning our next five AI-optimized facilities, and within the next five years, we aim to have all of our global operations running at net-zero emissions. We're not stopping here."

"And beyond that, we're planning to launch something even bigger: offering AI-as-a-Service and Sustainability-as-a-Service, built on the deep insights we've gained from transforming our own operations. This marks our shift from a manufacturing company to a strategic partner for industries worldwide. We've seen firsthand how powerful the combination of AI and sustainability can be - now, we're ready to help others unlock that same potential."

A few feet away, Steele watched the conversation, arms still folded, his expression unreadable. But then, just before turning away, he allowed himself a small, satisfied nod. Change had arrived. And ThermaDynamics was leading it.

For years, ThermaDynamics had been on the edge of transformation, struggling to convince the world, and itself, that the twin transformation of AI-driven sustainability wasn't just a corporate ideal, but an operational necessity. Today, there was no more doubt. The numbers, the technology, and the people all told the same story: this was the future.

A few weeks later, Richard Steele formally announced his retirement. After years of doubts and resistance, he had seen the transformation firsthand. In his final board meeting, he acknowledged the leadership team's vision. "I spent my last few years fighting change," he admitted. "But the truth is, this company is in better hands now than it ever was. And I wouldn't have it any other way."

Greaves looked at him, surprise flickering across his face. "You sure?"

Steele gave a small, knowing smile. "I got you this far, Thomas. Now it's your turn to take it the rest of the way."

Catalysts of Change

Just a few months after ThermaDynamics unveiled its first fully AI-optimized, net-zero emissions factory, a ripple effect was already beginning to take shape, far beyond its headquarters.

In Athens, Greece, Anna Xenaki, a young engineer with a passion for renewable energy and sustainable resource management, watched the company's success unfold. She had followed ThermaDynamics' journey closely, its transformation and its ultimate triumph in merging sustainability with digital innovation.

Sitting in a small solar energy research lab with a few colleagues, she pulled up the latest news article: 'ThermaDynamics Sets New Industry Standard: AI and Sustainability Prove to Be a Winning Formula.' Anna drew a breath, feeling a rush of excitement.

"We can do this," she said, turning to her team. "If they made it work at that scale, why can't we apply the same principles here?"

Their challenge wasn't manufacturing, but renewable energy integration, the complex problem of balancing wind, solar, and hydroelectric power with real-time demand and storage constraints. Inspired by ThermaDynamics, Xenaki and her team began drafting the blueprint for an AI-powered energy grid optimization system, one that could predict fluctuations in renewable power supply, optimize storage efficiency, and reduce energy waste across Greece's island communities, areas that struggled with energy stability due to outdated infrastructure.

Across the world, in Bangalore, India, Rohan Sharma, an AI researcher, was thinking along the same lines. Watching a panel discussion where Vikram Mehta and Elena Navarro outlined ThermaDynamics' transformation, he realized something profound; this wasn't just a corporate success story, it was a blueprint for global change.

For years, he had struggled to secure funding for AI-driven circular economy solutions in emerging markets. Investors had dismissed his ideas as too ambitious, too experimental. But now, with ThermaDynamics proving that AI could drive both profitability and sustainability, everything had changed. Sharma quickly revised his pitch deck, adding a new slide at the top: 'If They Did It, So Can We.'

Transformation Takeaways: Memo to Leadership

To: Thomas Greaves, CEO

From: Elena Navarro, Chief Sustainability Officer, and Vikram Mehta, Chief AI Officer

Date: August 2028

Subject: Lessons from Achieving Twin Transformation Victory

✅ What Worked

- **Company-wide alignment around twin transformation.**
  AI and sustainability were embedded into every department, from manufacturing and R&D to HR and sales, creating systemic cohesion and a unified strategic direction.
- **Successful pivot to subscription-based business model.**
  ThermaCloud™ and ICaaS generated significant recurring revenue, reduced client churn, and lowered adoption barriers, resulting in projected $300M+ ARR within 3 years.
- **Massive operational efficiency gains.**
  AI-driven optimization cut energy consumption by up to 40%, reduced production downtime, and drove $200M+ in cost savings annually.
- **Circular economy integration.**
  AI-enabled tracking, predictive waste modeling, and redesign-for-reuse reduced overproduction, reclaimed defective materials, and cut raw material use, saving millions and establishing a closed-loop supply chain.
- **Behavioral economics to influence clients.**
  Gamification, live cost dashboards, locked-in efficiency defaults, and incentive tiers shifted customer usage habits dramatically, reducing manual overrides by 68% and driving a 31% spike in energy efficiency.

- **Global scaling and localization strategy.**
  Regional customization of solutions (e.g., for historic EU buildings, emerging markets in Asia) and local partnerships enabled rapid international adoption with minimal friction.
- **Strategic external partnerships and open innovation.**
  The Sustainability Impact Fund and ecosystem model brought startups, suppliers, and competitors into ThermaDynamics' orbit, fueling faster innovation and sector-wide influence.
- **Investor confidence restored.**
  Key financial KPIs, recurring revenue streams, and market leadership in AI-driven building solutions led to a 15% stock surge and upgrades from major investment firms.

✖ What Didn't Work

- **Initial customer misuse of AI systems.**
  Clients frequently overrode AI recommendations, undermining energy efficiency goals and exposing the limitations of relying solely on tech without behavioral alignment.
- **Supplier pushback on circular economy demands.**
  Legacy suppliers resisted material tracking, cited high costs, and delayed retrofits, threatening progress on waste reduction.
- **High implementation costs for circular initiatives.**
  Upgrading sensors, systems, and supplier processes required substantial upfront investment, straining budgets and delaying ROI visibility.
- **Scaling challenges in complex global environments.**
  Regional regulations, infrastructure limitations, and cultural resistance made international deployment uneven and slower than projected in some markets.
- **Internal silos slowed execution.**
  Despite alignment at the top, operational silos persisted, especially between IT, sales, and R&D, requiring repeated interventions to sustain cross-functional execution.
- **Early hesitation on open innovation.**
  Delays in engaging with startups and external innovators initially

slowed down breakthroughs in materials science and clean energy integration.

📖 Lessons Learned

- **AI alone isn't enough; behavior must be designed.**
  The greatest energy gains came when AI was paired with behavioral nudges, gamification, and transparent incentives that aligned human behavior with technological optimization.
- **Sustainability must be embedded, not added.**
  Success came when sustainability became the metric by which all products, decisions, and strategies were evaluated, not when it was treated as a side objective.
- **The future of products is services.**
  Transitioning to subscription models (ThermaCloud™, ICaaS) created stability, deeper customer relationships, and predictable growth, marking a permanent shift from product sales to outcomes-as-a-service.
- **Circularity requires ecosystem thinking.**
  No company can build a circular economy alone. ThermaDynamics' shift from internal improvements to external ecosystem design was the key to system-level transformation.
- **Open innovation is essential at scale.**
  No matter how strong internal teams are, tapping into the global innovation ecosystem is critical to staying ahead in fast-moving fields like AI and sustainability.
- **Doubters can be won over by results.**
  Turning critics to endorsers proved that hard numbers, not persuasion alone, change minds. Demonstrated impact trumps ideology.

- **Sustainability is now a core business model.**
 What began as a compliance initiative became a competitive advantage, a product differentiator, and a long-term strategic asset, blending purpose and profit at scale.

Elena & Vikram

Epilogue

THE MERCURY PRIZE

Every ending writes its own echo.
The bold write what comes after.

The Grand Ballroom of the Majestic Hotel gleamed under the soft glow of crystal chandeliers. Tables adorned with white linen and golden centerpieces filled the space, occupied by the most influential figures in global business. The air buzzed with excitement and anticipation as the final award of the evening approached: The Mercury, named after the god of commerce and widely regarded as the Oscars of the business world.

Thomas Greaves adjusted his bow tie nervously as he glanced at Elena Navarro and Vikram Mehta seated beside him. The three of them, along with other key members of the ThermaDynamics leadership team, had made the journey to attend the prestigious ceremony. Their nomination for 'Best Transformation' had come as a surprise, though in retrospect, perhaps it shouldn't have.

"And now," announced Sophia Chen, the evening's host and CEO of Global Business Media, "for our final and, perhaps, most prestigious award of the evening: The Mercury for Best Business Transformation."

The massive screens displayed clips of the three finalists: a century-old automotive giant that had successfully pivoted to electric vehicles, a pharmaceutical company that had revolutionized its R&D through quantum computing, and ThermaDynamics, whose twin transformation in AI and sustainability had redefined industry standards.

"The winner of this year's Mercury Award for Best Business Transformation is..." Chen paused dramatically as she opened the envelope, "ThermaDynamics!"

The table erupted in celebration. Greaves clapped Mehta on the back while Navarro covered her mouth in shock. The spotlight found them as applause thundered through the ballroom.

"As part of our tradition," Chen continued once they had made their way to the stage, "the Mercury Award winners are invited to share their transformation journey with our audience. Please welcome Elena Navarro and Vikram Mehta of ThermaDynamics."

The crystal Mercury statue, a sleek figure with wings at its feet holding a caduceus, gleamed under the stage lights as Navarro took the podium first.

"Thank you," Navarro began, her voice steady despite her racing heart. "When Vikram and I joined ThermaDynamics three years ago, we had no idea we'd be standing here today."

She looked out at the sea of faces; there were CEOs, founders, investors, innovators, all waiting to hear the secret to their success.

"We were two executives with separate mandates: sustainability and artificial intelligence, that somehow became a singular mission. Tonight, we'd like to share the real story behind our transformation, not the polished version you might read in case studies, but the messy, challenging, sometimes painful journey that got us here."

Mehta stepped forward, adjusting the microphone. "Our first lesson was perhaps the most crucial, and it came from failure." He glanced at Navarro with a knowing smile. "**We learned that alignment must come before acceleration.**"

Navarro nodded. "When we started, AI and sustainability existed as parallel tracks. Vikram's team built brilliant AI systems focused on efficiency and automation. My team pushed for emissions reductions and circular economy initiatives. We were both successful in our silos, but the real transformation remained elusive."

"The turning point," Mehta continued, "came after a particularly disastrous quarterly review. Our chairman at the time, Richard Steele, called our efforts 'disconnected pet projects draining resources.' It stung because there was truth to it."

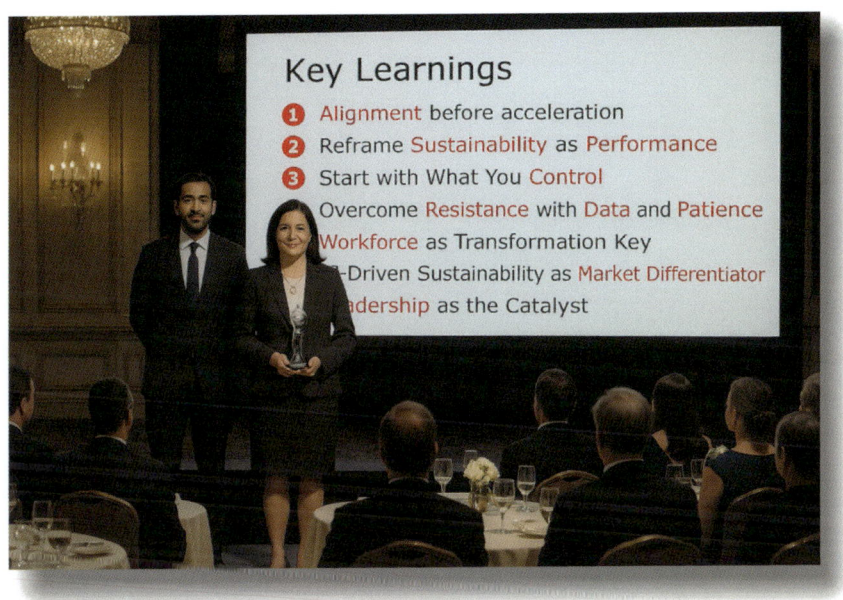

"So we made a radical decision," Navarro said. "We physically moved our teams together, created shared objectives, and rebuilt our AI models to optimize for sustainability alongside efficiency. The results were immediate and profound. The manufacturing digital twin, which had initially reduced energy consumption by 7%, reached 23% in early pilot results once sustainability parameters were integrated into its core architecture."

Mehta gestured to the audience. "For any company embarking on transformation, ask yourselves: are your strategic initiatives truly integrated, or are they competing priorities? True transformation happens at the intersection of initiatives, not in their separate successes."

Navarro continued. "Our second lesson was equally important: **reframe sustainability as a performance issue, not a compliance mandate.**"

She smiled as she recalled the memory. "There was a pivotal management meeting where our CFO, Katarina Svensson, was reviewing budgets. Our sustainability initiatives were categorized under 'Corporate Social Responsibility,' essentially a cost center. During that meeting, Vikram interrupted the presentation."

Mehta laughed. "I remember that day. I probably overstepped, but I couldn't help myself. I asked Katarina to recategorize our projects under 'Operational Excellence' instead."

"The room went silent," Navarro continued. "But that simple reframing changed everything. It wasn't just semantics; it reflected a fundamental truth we had discovered. When we positioned our AI-sustainability efforts as performance drivers rather than compliance costs, resistance melted away."

"The numbers spoke for themselves," Mehta added. "The Texas factory, our first major pilot, didn't just reduce emissions by 34%; it cut operational costs by 28%, reduced downtime by 28%, and improved product quality scores. Sustainability wasn't charity; it was good business."

"After that meeting," Navarro said, "we heard less about 'green premiums' and more about 'efficiency gains.' The question was no longer 'Can we afford to do this?' but rather 'Can we afford not to?'"

Mehta continued. "Our third lesson might seem contradictory to what I just said, but it was vital: **start with what you can control.**"

"Many companies fail in sustainability by trying to transform their entire value chain at once," he explained. "We made that mistake initially. We launched ambitious programs targeting Scope 1, 2, and 3 emissions simultaneously. We created complex supplier sustainability requirements and customer-facing green initiatives, all while our own house wasn't fully in order."

Navarro nodded. "The breakthrough came when we narrowed our focus. We concentrated first on our direct operations: factory energy use, production efficiency, material waste, and predictive maintenance, where we had complete control. Our AI systems created digital twins of every manufacturing process before we expanded outward."

"The strategy worked for two reasons," Mehta continued. "First, it gave us quick, measurable wins that built credibility. Second, it gave us the expertise and data to eventually influence our supply chain and customers from a position of proven success."

"By the time we approached our suppliers about reducing their carbon footprint," Navarro added, "we weren't making demands; we were sharing proven methodology. We could say, 'Here's exactly how we reduced our emissions by 40%, and here's how our AI systems can help you do the same.'"

Navarro straightened her posture as she moved to the next point. "Our fourth lesson was perhaps the most challenging: **overcoming resistance requires hard data and patience.**"

"Let me tell you about our Head of Operations," she said with a smile. "He was, to put it mildly, skeptical. He had spent thirty years perfecting ThermaDynamics' manufacturing process, and he viewed our AI-sustainability initiatives as a direct criticism of his life's work."

"He was also notorious for his red pen," Mehta added, earning knowing laughter from the audience. "Every proposal we submitted came back bleeding with critiques and objections. His favorite phrase was 'proven methods over shiny objects.'"

"We could have gone to our CEO and forced implementation," Navarro said, "but instead, we took a different approach. We chose one production line (the worst-performing one, actually) for a three-month pilot. We set clear, measurable KPIs: energy usage, production rate, defect rate, and maintenance costs."

"The results were irrefutable," Mehta said. "Energy consumption down 31%, throughput up 14%, defects down 23%, maintenance costs down 28%. Today, our Head of Operations is our biggest champion, not because we convinced him with rhetoric, but because the data did."

"Patience was crucial," Navarro emphasized. "Transformation doesn't happen overnight. It took eighteen months before skeptics fully embraced our vision. But when they did, their conversion was complete and their advocacy invaluable."

Mehta took center stage for the fifth lesson. "Perhaps our most important discovery was that the **workforce is the key to successful transformation.**"

"When we first introduced AI-driven automation and sustainability initiatives," he explained, "many employees feared job losses or impossible reskilling challenges. Others thought these were just corporate buzzwords that would eventually fade away."

"We learned quickly that the best technology and sustainability plans would fail without workforce buy-in," Navarro added. "We established clear communication about how these changes would reshape jobs, not eliminate them. We invested heavily in training programs, ensuring that everyone from factory workers to engineers had the skills to thrive in our new reality."

"One of our most successful initiatives," Mehta continued, "was the Transformation Champions program. We identified respected veterans in each department who understood both the old and new ways of working. These champions became the bridge between tradition and innovation."

"Maria Gonzalez in our Barcelona facility is a perfect example," Navarro said. "She had been with the company for twenty-two years, knew every aspect of production, and was initially skeptical of our AI systems. But once she saw their potential, she became our most effective advocate, training colleagues and even suggesting improvements to our models."

"By making employees part of the transformation rather than subjects of it," Mehta summarized, "we turned potential resistance into powerful momentum."

Navarro glanced at the timer, aware they were nearing the end of their allotted time. "Our sixth lesson might be the most commercially significant: **AI-driven sustainability can be your market differentiator.**"

"Initially, we applied AI only to internal factory efficiency," she explained. "But when we embedded AI-driven sustainability features into our products, such as self-optimizing climate control systems that reduced customer energy consumption by up to 38%, we unlocked entirely new revenue streams."

"The ThermaCloud platform," Mehta added, "transformed from an internal tool to a customer-facing service. It allowed clients to monitor and optimize their energy usage in real-time, predict maintenance needs, and demonstrate their own sustainability commitments."

"This created a virtuous cycle," Navarro said. "As our customers became more sustainable using our products, they demanded even more sustainable solutions from us and their other suppliers. What began as an internal transformation has sparked an industry-wide revolution."

Mehta stepped forward for their final point. "If there's one lesson that encompasses all others, it's this: **leadership is the catalyst for AI-driven sustainability.**"

"Our transformation was nearly derailed multiple times," he admitted, "not due to technical failures, but because of resistance at the leadership level. Some executives saw AI-driven sustainability as a distraction from core business priorities. Others worried about short-term financial impacts or operational disruptions."

"It took persistent leadership from our CEO," Navarro acknowledged, nodding toward Thomas Greaves in the audience, "along with a coalition of change agents throughout the company to push forward. Most importantly, they didn't rely on broad mandates or inspirational speeches alone."

"They built a coalition of supporters across departments," Mehta continued. "They modeled the right behaviors themselves. And they balanced urgency with patience, pushing for quick wins while understanding that full-scale adoption required cultural shifts."

"For any company embarking on this journey," Navarro concluded, "remember that AI and sustainability cannot be relegated to a Chief Sustainability Officer or AI team alone. It must be a top-level priority championed by the CEO and supported by the entire leadership team."

As they prepared to conclude, Mehta and Navarro looked at each other, silently acknowledging how far they had come.

"We stand before you tonight not as sustainability and AI experts, but as business transformation leaders," Navarro said. "The secret to our success wasn't just in the technologies we deployed or the environmental goals we set; it was in how we brought these elements together in service of business performance, customer value, and yes, planetary well-being."

Mehta lifted the crystal Mercury Award. "Three years ago, we set out to prove that AI could make ThermaDynamics more sustainable. Today, we've proven something more profound: AI-powered sustainability isn't just good practice; it's good business and the only way forward."

The audience rose in a standing ovation as Navarro and Mehta held the award together, a fitting symbol of the alignment that had been the foundation of their success.

In the front row, Thomas Greaves watched with pride, knowing that the true transformation of ThermaDynamics was just beginning. As Navarro had

whispered to him before taking the stage, "The best part is, we're just getting started."
The end.

About the Authors

Michael R. Wade

Michael Wade holds the TONOMUS Professorship in Digital and AI Transformation at the International Institute for Management Development (IMD) in Lausanne, Switzerland. He is also the Director of IMD's TONOMUS Global Center for Digital and AI Transformation. Previously, he was the Academic Director of the Kellogg-Schulich Executive MBA Program. He obtained Honours BA, MBA and PhD degrees from the Richard Ivey School of Business, University of Western Ontario, Canada.

Michael has published works on a variety of topics, including AI, digital business transformation, innovation, and information systems strategy. He has more than 100 articles and presentations to his credit in leading academic journals. He's published 11 books, more than thirty case studies, and appears frequently in the mainstream media.

Prior to *Twin Transformation*, his most recent books were *GAIN: Demystify GenAI for Office and Home* (2025), *Hacking Digital: Best Practices to Implement and Accelerate Your Business Transformation* (2022), *ALIEN Thinking: The Unconventional Path to Breakthrough Ideas* (2021), *Orchestrating Transformation*

(2019), and *Digital Vortex* (2016). His books have been translated into multiple languages.

Michael was inaugurated into the Swiss Digital Shapers Hall of Fame in 2021.

Michael has lived and worked in Britain, Canada, Japan, Norway, and Costa Rica. He currently resides with his family in Switzerland.

Konstantinos V. Trantopoulos

Konstantinos Trantopoulos is a Research Fellow at the International Institute for Management Development (IMD) in Lausanne, Switzerland. He holds a PhD in Strategic Management from ETH Zurich, where he received the ETH Medal, as well as an MSc and BSc in Applied Mathematics from the National Technical University of Athens, and a Certificate of Advanced Studies in International Organizations from the University of Zurich. He has been a visiting researcher at the University of California and MIT.

Konstantinos focuses on strategy, firm performance, business transformation, and the organizational impact of AI. His early career experience in corporate development and strategy consulting informs both his scholarship and work with organizations. He frequently advises Fortune 500 companies, private equity firms, and government agencies, and remains active in the start-up scene. His research and thought leadership have been featured in mainstream media and leading outlets such as *MIS Quarterly*, *California Management Review*, *Industry and Innovation*, and *MIT Sloan Management Review*.

Konstantinos is a dual citizen of Greece and Switzerland. He has lived in Greece, Germany, France, and the United States, and currently resides in Switzerland. He grew up in Athens, Greece.